· · · · · · · · · ·

My Vices Collide

A Celebration of Being a Little Messed Up

· · · · · · · · ·

My Vices Collide

A Celebration of Being a Little Messed Up

Sharla Dawn Gorder

Wonpontime Publishing
216 Ariola Dr.
Pensacola Beach, FL 32561

Cover design and illustrations by Jem Sullivan
Book design by Casey Braun
Author photograph by Janna Marie Rasch
Wonpontime logo by Taylor Gorder

My Vices Collide contains essays previously published
on Sharladawn.com, as well as new material.

ISBN 978-0-9976551-0-0
2 4 6 8 9 7 5 3 1

Author's note: This is a work of creative nonfiction.
The events are portrayed to the best of my memory.
Some names and identifying characteristics have been changed and
events reordered or compressed.

Visit the author's website at Sharladawn.com

For Ted
my Stoker, my husband, my hero
—my *only one only one*.

Table of Contents

Hello There

My Vices Collide 3
Caveat 5
Sharla Dawn 7

Outside - to Play

Arts and Crafts – The Making of a Wreath 19
Balance 23
Cottonwood 33
Stoker 39

Creatures Great and Small and in My Head

Wanted: SWF 51
Fido 61
Curious George Meets King Kong 71
LOL 81

Raised in a Barn - by Wolves

Myles and the Tapir 89
Not Tonight, I Have a Headache 93
Don't Take Your Dolphin to School 99
Triceratops and Tissues 107

It's a Girl Thang

Horriblariousness 121
Coiffus Interruptus 125
A Bladder Matter 131
Heavier Things 135

Flaw Slaw

Spontaneous Instruction 147

Twig 151

My Apologies.. 165

Shallows 169

Messy Mortals

Moonshadow.. 173

ESM.. 179

Flower Power and the Mean Girls 183

Schizophrenic Sky.. 197

Redemption

Surge.. 203

Morning Mourning... 209

Do Tell.. 211

All Told 221

Dear James 227

God-ish

Six-pack 237

Hey God.. 245

More 255

Jesus Pancake... 261

OMG.. 263

Bye Now

Ba Dum Tshh!! 273

I am Sand... 277

Every Ship that Sails 283

Hello
There

. . . .

My Vices Collide

My vices have always collided—right there in the middle of my day when I'd suddenly be forced to stop drinking coffee so that I could start drinking wine. Or I'd be in the middle of lecturing one of the boys when Ted walked in from work, and I couldn't wait to *start* nagging *him*. And lately, I've had to interrupt a *Big Bang* binge to Crush Candy on my iPad. It's exhausting keeping up with all my vices. You'd think I'd be better at it by now. I've had a lot of practice.

But I'm a little messed up, you see. Not hopelessly ruined, mind you. Just a little bit broken and a wee bit bemused. I've spent a lot of emotion and energy apologizing for that, or otherwise trying to compensate, disguise or deny my numerous peccadillos.

I once had a friend who apologized for a plant. She noticed the solitary dead leaf on her ficus as we chatted on her sofa. She plucked the offending foliage, simultaneously apologizing to me, for *what* I'm not quite sure—or maybe she was apologizing to the plant. It wasn't clear. Either way, I decided to forgive her. I think the plant did too.

And then, in a flash of divine inspiration, I decided to just go ahead and forgive myself too. Why not? And while I was at it, why not have a little fun with it?

We are all, every one of us, what I call "messy mortals." And while there are clearly times when vices must be acknowledged, eradicated and atoned for, the vast majority of the things I beat myself up about could just as easily be celebrated.

So, the plant has a brown leaf. It has 4,000 pretty green ones, too. So, I can pinch way more than an inch. I can also swim out to the second sandbar and back without my water wings. Maybe my house will never grace the cover of *Metropolitan Home*, but neither will it be featured on an upcoming episode of *Hoarders* on TLC.

Yes, I locked my keys in my car again; I set the Thanksgiving turkey on fire; I wore my pants inside out all day; I ran over my iPad—twice; I threw up in my own purse.

I have also raised happy boys, relished precious relationships and enjoyed grand adventures all over the globe. I've shown up for work on time, learned to play the piano, and helped care for my aging parents. I've cherished hundreds of friends, read thousands of books, traveled millions of miles.

Oh, but it's so much more fun to write about that *one* time I accidentally threw up in my purse. I am, I confess, among the messiest of mortals, as everyone in that Chevy Suburban would attest. And I have lived to tell the tale.

You are holding it in your hands.

Caveat

This book won't make you rich or skinny or popular. If it could, Lord knows, I'd be rich and skinny and popular because I would have had to have figured all that out in order to tell you how it's done. I haven't figured all that out. Just so you know.

This book probably won't be discussed on Oprah's network or reviewed by Michiko Kakutani for *The New York Times*. Your grandkids won't study it in high school. It won't ever be a major motion picture, coming soon to a theater near you, starring, let's say, Jenna Elfman, as me.

It isn't really a memoir; but neither is it fiction. It isn't "serious literature," but it isn't *trash lit* either. It isn't an autobiography, a comedy, a romance or a self-help book, though there are elements of each of those genres in these pages.

This is a *story* book. Without the pictures. Well, actually, the pictures are there, magnificent ones, but I've *written* them in *words* for your imagination to draw. It's more fun that way. Your imagination is a great artist.

What you have here are *stories*. True stories about life, mine in particular. Nothing more highfalutin than that.

I hope that's enough to keep you entertained for the next 284 pages, because, well, that's why I compiled them. To entertain you. If I manage to inspire, amuse and *move* you, well, that's even better. But it's not required. Actually, nothing is required. You will not be tested.

This book is a collection of true, inspirational essays about being all things to all people at all times, and failing beautifully. You can trust me; I am an expert in this field. I am a woman and a mom and a daughter and a wife and a sister and a friend and an employee and an employer and a writer and a yogi and a nutcase. I have succeeded and failed, risen and fallen, loved and lost, soared and slithered. I'll give you all the gory details. I'll give you all the glory details, too.

But I won't be throwing anyone under any buses. I thought long and hard about this and decided that, as hard as I can be on my*self*, I will not disparage others. And that includes my husband, and, of course, my kids. I won't even bad-mouth the person who was really mean to me and deserves it. (Well, at least not by name.)

So, if, while reading about my peeps, you get the impression that my husband is perfect, my kids are choir-boys, and all my friends are saints, please consider your own loved ones, and rest assured that mine are just as quirky and messed up as yours. But I'd like to keep them around, warts and all if you please. And divulging their secrets, while great for selling books, has no socially-redeeming value. And, you should know, I'm all about redemption. And value. May you find a little of both in these pages.

Sharla Dawn

Ihave always wanted to be *her*—ever since I was a little kid. There are references to this in my diaries going back nearly fifty years. She was the epitome of loveliness to me, of grace, of tranquility. She was kind and resourceful. She was elegant and natural, and moved unselfconsciously through her world—even in a bikini. She was the "She-sells-seashells-on-the-seashore" girl. I wanted to be her. I still do. Such lofty ambitions.

I grew up in the Deep South on an island. Well, on a diamond-shaped peninsula overlooking an island, a barrier island called Santa Rosa, in the far northwest corner of the Florida Panhandle. I am the youngest of three. My little town, my peninsula, has the prettiest name, especially appealing to a She-sells-seashells-on-the-seashore girl. It is called Gulf Breeze, and it's as lovely as its name. My childhood home was on a palmetto-lined road called *Dolphin*. Our street number just happened to be the same as the chapter and verse of my favorite passage in the Bible. My best friends lived on streets named Sunset and Shoreline and Camellia and Magnolia.

Across the Three-Mile-Bridge to the north of Gulf Breeze was the city of Pensacola. To the south across the one-mile Bob Sikes Bridge was "that beach" (as my Dad contemptuously referred to it)—that glistening treasure chest of decadence and delight. I came of age, as they say, on Pensacola Beach in the '60s and '70s.

At ten, I was a wannabe hippie, and at twelve, a devout disciple of the burgeoning Jesus Movement. At fifteen, I discovered boys and piña coladas and anorexia. At sixteen, I moved out of the house on Dolphin Street to "that beach" with two girlfriends. At seventeen, I moved to Costa Rica for nine months with my friend, Karen, ostensibly to study Spanish and teach English.

And yes, I did have parents. Two of them. And they loved me and provided for me. But if "helicopter" parenting is one extreme on the parenting spectrum, I'd have to say mine were on the other end—more the aircraft-carrier type of folks. I always had a big safe place to land (or crash). Mom and Dad weren't always the most engaged, but they had their reasons. Grown-up reasons that I didn't understand and didn't care to. I had a car, a job at the mall and no real curfew. What more could a venturesome teenager want?

At nineteen, I was already done with school *and* my lovely little town. I had taken the fast track through high school and college and was desperate to get away from the very place I would eventually be desperate to return to.

But to come back, I had to go away. Way away.

"My wound is geography," Pat Conroy writes in his powerful novel *The Prince of Tides:* "It is also my anchorage, my port of call." I would first read those words years later as a Pan Am flight attendant—my first job after graduating college—strapped into the jump-seat of a 747SP headed for Sydney, or Maui or Fiji. Though I don't remember exactly where I was headed, I was far, far away from "my anchorage, my port of call." Did my heart know, even then, that I would return to that sandbar in the sea?

I couldn't have, at least not on a conscious level. But the blood in my veins was saltier than most, and my eyes were always drawn to deep greens and blues. I found serenity in raging thunderstorms. My feet were cranky in shoes.

Still, for the privilege of traveling the world, I wore shoes—and with a minimum two-inch heel. That was the rule, and there were many more. Pan Am's dress code was meticulous and strictly enforced. Seashell girl was now obliged to wear, not only shoes, but also pantyhose and makeup. But that was only part of it. I was required to learn some really important stuff, too—like how to evacuate 400 screaming passengers from a blazing 747; how to best position and stifle a bomb at 35,000 feet; how to converse with a hijacker in a bad mood; and how to keep the pilots awake on a 15-hour flight to Dhahran (lots of jokes).

But most importantly, I learned to love the world, and all the diverse and crazy people in it—*eventually*. It would take some time. Having grown up on an island in the South, I often felt like a dolphin at a ski resort. The six-week Pan Am training course was in Honolulu. That adjustment was easy enough because of the palm trees and all, but my very first domicile with Pan Am was (drum roll, please) *New York City*. My first work assignment—or "line"—took me to Narita, Japan. Then Nairobi, Kenya. Then Detroit.

I had moved from Gulf Breeze, Florida (population, 5,478) to New York, New York (population, 7 million-plus). Within the year, I would visit every continent except Antarctica. That first year, when I wasn't working, I hid out alone in my 350 square-foot studio apartment on the fringe of Spanish Harlem. I just knew that everyone in the city could see that I was a dolphin, and dolphins were not welcome at Bloomingdale's in the late '70s. Maybe they are now.

A couple of years later, I left New York for London, chasing a boy across the Atlantic. Less than a year after that, the relationship took a rather sinister turn, and I found myself homeless in the cobbled streets of Twickenham. Pan Am granted me a hardship transfer out of London to Los Angeles. I ended up fleeing the country like a refugee.

Ah, L.A. At last, a place a dolphin could feel at home. The water was too cold there, and it confused me that the ocean was always to the west of me instead of to the south. But there was salt in the air. It made the smog bearable. And there were palm trees, impossibly tall ones lining Pacific Coast Highway. There were new friends. There were more disastrous romances. There was the whole 1980s life-in-the-fast-lane-Southern-California-scene.

I loved it. I stayed the whole decade. I even remember some of it.

The next time I chased a boy down I didn't have so far to travel—just up the coast a ways. I met my husband, Ted, on a flight (yes, isn't that romantic?) from Los Angeles to Sydney, Australia. When we met, he had been living in Melbourne for the better part of a year and was just finishing up a project for his accounting firm. When he moved back to Washington, we did the long distance dance for a couple of years getting a great deal of use from my travel benefits and his frequent flier miles. That got old.

I moved to Seattle. Have you ever seen a dolphin in Birkenstocks? Ha! Neither had they. But, hey, it was Seattle; they were cool with it. (Just so you know, Seattleites are cool with just about everything—as long as you recycle, and know that a *Grande* Double Ristretto Half-Soy Nonfat Decaf Organic Frappuccino is actually *smaller* than the *Vente* version, you're good.)

I was already in my 30s when I married Ted, the love of my life. I had never even been engaged before. I had been a staunch serial monogamist since puberty, never going more than 35 or 40 seconds between boyfriends, but this boy—and oh, how he looks like such a beautiful *boy* in our wedding photos—this boy had swept me off my feet, navy blue pumps and all. I'd always been happier barefoot anyway. And what goes best with *barefoot* to a newlywed from the Deep South?

Pregnant—the second best thing that ever happened to me. Twice. Myles was born eight weeks early. Taylor, we had to go in and get.

The next twenty years are kind of a blur—a "brutiful" blur as Glennon Melton would put it. She writes that "Life is equal parts brutal and beautiful." I can imagine no arena more illustrative of that *brutifulness* than parenting. I highly recommend it.

But I can't say it was easy. When Myles was born, Ted and I knew that one of us would have to quit our jobs since both of our careers required extensive international travel. It only made sense that the one with the lactating breasts would stay home. I cried as I penned my letter of resignation to United (by that time, Pan Am had sold their routes and employees to other airlines before going under.) My supervisor cried, too.

There's something about being a mom that makes a mom miss *her* mom. I was so very far away from home with my babies. In those early years Ted would be gone to Warsaw, or Wellington, or Dubai for weeks at a time. I stayed home alone with our little boys—a privilege and a hardship. Dolphins live in pods. They *must*, or they perish. I became lonely. I became depressed. I became my mom.

I wrote a song as I emerged from those post-partum days. The first lines were: "Days came down to marking time/Too much darkness, too much wine/Nights I fell alone to sleep/Prayed the Lord my soul to keep …" And He did. He kept my soul safe. The dark drape of depression began to part, and with every pull of the cord, more light came in, more warmth in that cold, wet Seattle winter.

But I had to pull the cord. It wasn't the first time I'd been challenged to take action to protect myself from my own pathology. And it wasn't the last time. In my gene pool, among the women especially, anxiety and depression are treacherous, muddy riptides, and they were already carrying my own mother out to that vast sea where her mother before her had perished.

It is so hard to reach for anything—even a line that's dangling right there in your face—when anxiety has morphed into dark depression and every choice seems impossible. I remember standing at the refrigerator in my chenille robe and tube socks—a screaming baby on my shoulder and another playing in the Tupperware cabinet. I wanted orange juice but felt utterly overwhelmed by the gallon of milk and the bowl of blueberries that were in front of it. I would have to move them *both*. Aw, screw it. It couldn't possibly be worth all that effort.

But the screaming baby and the Tupperware toddler had other plans for me. And God had other plans for me—"to prosper me and not to harm me." I vaguely remembered those words from my evangelical adolescence. They were true that morning.

They are true now.

They will be true tomorrow.

I have been lost many times in my life. I'll tell you all about it. I have been found the exact same number of times. I'll tell you all about that too. And about how I came to trade my Birkenstocks for flip-flops, and eventually for bare toes in the sand. I'll tell you how I came back to that island in the Gulf of Mexico, to resume my rightful place on the shoreline, bent over the beach, searching for seashells. I like the broken ones best now.

I was a broken one when we moved back to Gulf Breeze from Seattle. Marriage was hard. Parenting was even harder. My own parents, still living on their farm just over the Florida/Alabama border, were struggling—my Mom in a plunging spiral of dementia, Dad lost in sympathetic confusion and loneliness. Even my brother and sister seemed a little like strangers to me at first. I had been away for nearly twenty years.

Ted and I and our boys had come back for the sunshine, and to be closer to my parents in their final years. And though it was *my* hometown, Ted assimilated more easily than I. He went *out* in the community to build his consulting business. I stayed *inside* our house building blanket forts. It took *me* some time.

Again, I had to *make* myself reach up and pull the cord, part the drapes a little. Florida had delivered on the sunshine; it was there right outside my window, but I had to let it in.

For me *then*, as now, pulling the cord has meant so many things—all of them actions. I would have to *do* stuff—move the milk and blueberries. I would to have to get out of my house *and my head* and engage with others. I joined a gym, a book club, a mommy-and-me play group for each of the boys.

I began to reestablish old relationships—with my siblings, Sandee and Jem; my niece, Jenna; and a few childhood best friends, Räna and Karen and Betty. I made new best friends—Anna, Vanessa, Michele. Later, Kelly, Lynas and Dawn.

After the boys started school, I got a part-time job traveling around the United States a weekend or two a month working as a site coordinator for a company that organized medical conferences. During the week I also worked a few hours as a personal trainer and aerobics instructor at my gym. I got to be home when Myles and Taylor got off the bus in the afternoons. They made a mommy out of me, and I can't thank them enough for teaching me how to love with utter abandon. It's my best quality.

I raised our boys. I wrote stories. I played the piano. I cooked. I read books. Ted worked and traveled. A lot.

We had built a beautiful house in a prestigious neighborhood in the middle of town. I decorated and shopped and entertained. A lot.

We lost that beautiful house in that prestigious neighborhood when the high-tech company that Ted consulted for down-sized in the dot-com recession, and he was abruptly let go. I mourned and drank and moped. A lot.

That's the way I do most things. Excessively.

We sold most anything we thought we could live without—which was about everything but the boys and cats—and moved to a little house down the highway.

We started over. In our mid-40s. Our joint income that first year, for our little family of four, was around twelve thousand dollars. But even that cumulonimbus cloud of sudden unemployment had a silver lining. Ted was home now. With us. No longer working "for" us, he was home and working *with* us.

He still is. Fifteen years later. We built a new business, a solid family, a good life. It was really, really hard (and is). It was really, really fun (and is). We got lost again. We got found. A few years ago we traded the little house down the highway for a little house on "that beach."

My toes are in the sand again. *Ahhh.* And you wouldn't believe the bounty of seashells on the beach today—three inches deep in places. The Gulf has been turbulent all week. The shells are broken. *They've gone through a lot to get here.* I get that.

I do *so* love the broken ones.

Sharla Dawn Gorder

Outside to Play

Arts and Crafts – The Making of a Wreath

Spring has come early this year. After a tumultuous winter of torrential rains, giant waves, and punishing winds, the Gulf is finally relaxing in its bed. It's like a postcard out there this morning—*"Greetings from Florida, the Land of Sunshine."* Yes, there is a warm abundance of that this morning, and now—after all those storms—there is a bounty of seashells too.

That's the part I like best—the shells. As a self-proclaimed she-sells-seashells-on-the-seashore girl, I *live* for days like these. The truth is, though, I've never been much good at sales—I'm actually more comfortable being the she-*shares*-seashells-on-the-seashore girl. What I have I will always share with you. And what I have *now* are an abundance of broken shells. They are beautiful.

For the longest time I only picked up the whole ones. I searched and searched for perfect, unchipped seashells after storms. As a young teenager I would ride my bike out to Fort Pickens Point from my house in Gulf Breeze—a good 15 miles—to search for shells. I still remember the first time I found a Scotch bonnet, my favorite of all beach treasures. I was combing the beach, sunburned and thirsty and dreading the long ride home when I rounded the Point and stopped to look out over the pass. I sat down in a little tide pool, and dug my fingers into the sand and scooped up a dripping handful of shards and shells and quartz. And there it was—no bigger than a ping pong ball, helmet-shaped, bleached bright white, and perfectly formed—my first Scotch bonnet.

I must have been 14 or 15 then, and to this day some 40 years later, I have only found three or four more whole Scotch bonnets. Unbroken shells are rare, especially after a season of pounding surf. Only the shiny olives, the sturdy cylindrical shells common to this area, seem to consistently wash up on the beach whole, and maybe that's only because they are so thick, and closed in around themselves—protected. But I usually leave *them* be—for the tourists to pick up and take home.

When we first moved back to Florida after being away for nearly twenty years, I couldn't wait to get back out on the beach with my net bag and laminated shell card. The boys were too young to enjoy the hunt, and too, well—little *boy*ish—to appreciate the delicate treasures I sought.

But Jenna was not. My little niece had grown up while I was away. She was no longer the snaggletoothed "cutie patootie," who screamed like you were gouging her eyeballs out with scissors every time you washed her hair in the outdoor shower. No, she had elongated, and simmered down, and had become almost mermaidish in both appearance and disposition.

At 15, she was tall and tan and lissome and lithe and could swim out to the second sandbar and be on her way back before I could put my seashells down. And she could spot an unbroken sand-dollar no bigger than a dime, without even bending over.

Shelling with her was like diving with Jaques Cousteau. Jenna had lived her whole life on the island. The Gulf flowed in her veins.

Jenna always let me have the unbroken ones. I found my second Scotch bonnet with her one day in early October out in front of her house. It was the only one I took home that day, but Jenna had a pocketful of broken whelks and augers, conchs and coquinas.

Maybe she knew something I didn't.

Today, I like the broken ones better too. I'm making a wreath of broken whelks. My astonishingly creative friend, Alana, made one a couple of years ago and let me borrow it for the holidays. It brought me such delight that I decided to make one myself. Only *mine* will be in the shape of a peace sign.

Every shell in Alana's wreath is broken, and that's what makes it so beautiful. If the shells weren't broken open at the top, I wouldn't be able to see inside. The wreath would have less depth and complexity. And it is the fact that they are *all* broken in some way that makes this work of art so profound to me.

We are all broken open in some way. Every last one of us. And that's a good thing. More light and air and truth get in that way. When I see a broken shell, I don't think, "Uh-Oh, this is chipped, I need to fix it." No, *now* I look out over the Gulf and think, "Wow, this little treasure has been through a lot to get here. It's beautiful."

You too, little treasure, have been through a lot to get here, and you are beautiful. I know this because I have met so many of you and talked with you and laughed with you and cried with you. I am drawn to you, broken ones, because I am broken too, and we are in this wreath together.

The places where one shell is broken fit the contours of another shell that is whole on that side but perhaps chipped on the other. Then that space accommodates the next shell in the wreath, and so on and so on, and that is how a community is built. We nestle together in our shared struggles and triumphs and make something lovely of our world.

I may not look chipped and cracked and hollowed out to you at first glance. (I clean up pretty good.) But I will tell you this: It wasn't until I allowed myself to be broken open, to be honest with myself and entirely vulnerable and truthful with someone I trusted, that my life changed in ways I could never have imagined. And to my utter astonishment, I learned that *that* person was broken too, and that *we had a wreath to make.* Speak up if you are struggling. There's a space for you in the circle.

A space for you in our peace sign. This brokenness, this shared vulnerability is the key to my serenity—my peace of mind. I'm gathering shells on the beach to make my peace wreath. It will take hundreds and hundreds, but I'm in no hurry. There will always be a fresh supply of broken shells on the shore. Of that I'm sure.

This morning I went out with my little shell bag and headed east along the shore break. I had walked for less than a minute when I came to the first small patch of crunched up shells. They were whispering to me as the tiny waves washed over them. I crouched down and the first shell I reached for—I am not making this up—was a Scotch bonnet, broken almost beyond recognition.

It is still my favorite.

Balance

We like to get outside and balance on stuff. I don't know why that is or what it means, if anything, but it seems to run through my lineage—my Dad, myself and my son—three generations of casual balancers. There's Daddy, all muscled and tan in the photo (circa 1947) standing comfortably as though waiting for a bus—except upside-down, on his hands. Then, there's me, half a century later, relaxing happily on my blue paddle board on a green sea—on my head. And this latest picture is of Myles, perched high in the limb of a mossy scrub oak, hands in prayer position at his heart in the yoga pose called *tree*, balanced on one foot.

I stumbled across all three of these snapshots this week, and I couldn't help but notice how comfortable all three of us looked in these unlikely postures, how relaxed we each were, and how odd it might seem to others—those who don't have this need to balance on stuff—that we three find some kind of calm exhilaration in the challenge of balancing our bodies in unconventional ways.

Balance. What a loaded word these days. Not just something tightrope walkers need, balance has become the prescription for nearly everything that ails us. Finances a mess? *Balance your budget*. Emotions in turmoil? *Balance your hormones*. Body bloated and sluggish. *Balance your diet.* Relationships failing? *Balance your priorities.*

A few years ago, I sought out a psychologist to help me through a tangled time. And yes, the Rx I was handed was *balance*. The prescription itself is a metaphor, and frankly, one that I had a hard time buying into. Though I understood the implied symbolism, my mind kept returning to the circus and those fearless funambulists with their impossibly thin cables and long poles, inching timidly across oblivion on bare feet. Talk about stressful. That just seems really hard—despite the fact that I kinda like balancing on stuff, and I'm happiest when I'm shoeless. I'm just not too keen on the consequence of error being death or dismemberment.

So we had to take the *balance* concept in a different direction. My therapist got right on it. Metaphors were her specialty, and that was lucky for me because I love a good analogy. She suggested I imagine half a dozen or so bowls, baskets, or other vessels of my choosing, all different, but all capable of holding stuff. I was then to imagine that each—cereal bowl, say—represents a fundamental aspect of my life for that day. One for family. One for work. One for fun. One for self-care. And so on and so forth.

My mission, should I choose to accept it, was to then make deposits in every bowl every day. This actually seemed like a good strategy for me, as my default all-or-nothing mentality usually has me flooding one bowl with gallons of effort while all the other bowls remain dry.

I liked the concept. So much so that I went home and played around on my new computer designing power point slides of various metaphorical receptacles into which I could distribute my time and talents.

The first one was coffee cups. I love everything about coffee—the smell, the taste, the buzz, the feel of the warm cup in my sleepy hands. Coffee is a lovely morning ritual and especially pleasant on the mornings when my husband discreetly places a steaming cup on my nightstand as I rouse.

My completed masterpiece depicted a dozen cups including a giant mug sculpted to look like a person's profile with the handle formed by the tongue curving up to touch the nose. It reminded me of my late Aunt Mickey who performed that trick herself at Christmas and Thanksgiving dinners. That was the cup I'd designate for all the fun, whimsical stuff.

I also included the basic, utilitarian, white roadside-diner-style cup and saucer, for the routine housework and maintenance chores. Of course, there was a shiny silver travel mug, a wide, shallow latte bowl with coordinating saucer, and a tiny blue demitasse cup with its own itty bitty spoon. The latter I'd use for the stuff I really didn't want to do, as it would only hold a couple of ounces and take minimal effort to fill up.

And, *voilà*, there was my template. I posted one copy above my desk, one on the island in the kitchen, and even put one in my car. Then I went about my day, ever mindful of my goal—to *apportion* my energies.

After implementing this process for a few days, I found I was indeed quite busy and active, but my productivity didn't seem to be improving. In my fervor to keep from overflowing one cup or neglecting another, I found myself flitting from activity to activity aimlessly, like a hummingbird with Alzheimer's.

I concluded it must be my template's fault. Back to the drawing board. What image might inspire me to achieve the balance I so desired? I sat at my computer watching the cursor blink, and then—*Eureka!* I had it.

Martini shakers!

This template was awesome. I had, just a few years earlier, developed a rather pretentious and reckless fascination with all things *martini*. Although it was fun while it lasted, it couldn't last too long, as I discovered that I had a limited number of brain cells to squander. Fortunately, though, I had retained a few relics of my obsession, including a pretty little collection of cocktail shakers.

And so there it was, my second visual aid, a colorful mélange of martini mixers: retro, contemporary, classic, metal, acrylic, ceramic. How fun, funky and festive! It made me happy just to look at it. And thirsty.

It didn't take me long to realize that the "party hearty" subtext of my latest compilation was distracting me from the *serious business* of balancing out my life. So I tossed back the dregs of my third Cosmo and headed back to the drawing board. A little deflated. I was discouraged, but not yet ready to throw in the towel.

I was stumped. Alas, what could *possibly* adequately represent a proper repository for my precious time and extensive talents? Back to Google images. How about woven baskets? Love those— but nah, boring. Pocketbooks? Could be cute, maybe. Porcelain pottery? Artsy. A possibility. Baby bottles? Probably not. A little too sentimental. Hmmm. I sat there feeling a little cranky when it came to me in a flash of ornery inspiration. I had it!

Toilets! Yes, *toilets*: potties, johns, crappers, heads, commodes, loos, latrines, porcelain gods, cans. That's where all my time and talent seemed to end up anyway. Why not have the appropriate visual aid?

It is clearly no coincidence that I was in a *pissy* mood when I started this, my final pictorialization. I have to say, however, that my attitude improved appreciably just a few minutes into my *Google images* search for "unique toilets." While most were far too vulgar to include in this PG-rated project, I did have some fun perusing potties. Who would have thought there would be such variety? I finally settled on a loo made entirely of ice, a scary clown-head head, a trombone urinal, a toilet tricycle and a Jaws john.

When I showed my masterpieces to my therapist the following week, she just smiled with that, "And how does this make you feel?" expression, and let me fill in my own blanks. Thank you, Elaine.

I guess I should mention that the circumstances which precipitated my visit to a therapist were dire. I had, in the preceding months, been abruptly forced by the illnesses of both of my parents to take on the role of caretaker, struggling frantically along with my siblings and husband to keep my mom and dad alive as they moved in and out of the unfamiliar, ironically *in*hospitable landscape of hospitals, physical rehab units, and assisted-living facilities. I was drinking too much and sleeping and eating too little. I was at odds with other family members and feeling disconnected from my husband and kids. It was a somber time.

Of course I felt off balance, out of sorts, unstable. It seemed my daddy was dying. My mom was lost in the depths of dementia and eventually came to live with me for a while. My relationships were strained and brittle. I was exhausted.

So what the hell was I doing on the computer searching for pictures of pretty coffee cups, cute martini shakers and funny toilets?

I was finding my balance. Oddly enough, of all the aspects of my life which were out of whack at that time, it seemed that my sense of humor (of whimsy, of playfulness) was the one that I most desperately needed to reconnect with.

Balance is actually an intuitive thing—in the universe, in nature, and in me. And while it is surely appropriate, and often fun, to *work* at different aspects of it at times, I'm finding that if I'm still enough to sense, quiet enough to listen, and patient enough to wait, I will often naturally ease into my balance without a struggle.

One of my very favorite parables is the Taoist story that tells of an old man who accidentally falls into a river and is swept away by the rapids into a giant, crushing waterfall. Onlookers, certain that the man has plummeted to his death, are stunned to see him emerge downstream unharmed. When questioned about his survival, the man replies, "I went up when the water went up and down when the water went down."

Those of us who live by the ocean also know that the only way to survive a rip current is to first go *with it*, and then calmly swim parallel to the shore until the tide releases you. Flailing against it, no matter how strong or trained or well-intentioned you are, won't get you safely to shore.

I know, of course, that there is much more to leading a "balanced" life than merely surviving—more to being balanced than not falling down. There is grace in balance. Look at a beautifully expressed triangle pose in yoga, or a surfer dropping in on a glassy wave. That balance is lovely, even exhilarating, and yes, requires time and practice to achieve.

But there can and should be *joy* in that pursuit, as long as it is grounded in acceptance of what is. Accept the waterfall that is your reality.

Yesterday, as I worked on this piece, I was thwarted at every turn by distractions and interruptions. In a one-hour period, I counted twelve intrusions into my sacred writing space. Finally, I just typed, "Ah, screw it," and resigned myself to the waterfall.

I had had an agenda: "Write for two hours." But it just wasn't gonna happen. That particular coffee cup, martini shaker, or toilet bowl, wasn't brimming with accomplishment as I had planned, but neither was it empty. And interestingly, most of the other little vessels were filling up as well. I had unwittingly contributed to my "spirit" cup with a spontaneous discussion with Myles in the kitchen about free will. I had deposited compassion into my "friendship" cup when a friend called and needed some encouragement. I had worked on finances for Taylor's tuition, scaled an Everest of laundry, emptied the dishwasher, and accomplished several other household tasks that currently constitute a large part of my "work" cup.

My compulsive nature has often driven me to throw the baby out with the bathwater any time my plans get interrupted or revised. I do it with diets and exercise plans. I do it with small projects and big goals. I tend to hyper-focus on one thing until I'm good and sick of it. At that point, any intrusion is the perfect excuse to quit.

But I didn't do that yesterday, because I had my coffee cups to remind me that my life is multidimensional. If my demitasse cup stays dry on Wednesday, and my travel mug overflows, well, there's always Thursday, and then the whole weekend right around the corner to tend to the others. It will all even out, if I flow *with* it instead of against it.

Of course, there are times when distractions just have to be minimized in order to follow through on commitments or meet deadlines. Sometimes that roadside diner cup simply must be filled by the end of the work day on Friday. But usually, for me, an intransigent approach to my day—while perhaps enabling me to get a story written ahead of schedule, or the spices alphabetized—doesn't allow me to align myself with core values that are important to me on the deepest level. For example, I get *into* trouble and *out of* balance almost any time my "busyness" doing *things* causes me to neglect *people*.

I remember, with clarity and regret, an afternoon when Taylor was about three, and I just *had* to get the kitchen grout bleached, the swing-set dried off, the litter boxes changed, and a dozen other chores checked off my list. I think somebody "important" must have been coming over with their kid for a playdate. I had picked Taylor up from pre-school and was scurrying around the house like a manic mouse in a maze as Taylor toddled along behind me. I was hustling down the driveway to get the mail when Taylor caught up with me. He flung his pudgy arms around my legs and said, "Mommy, stop moving."

Sharla, *stop moving* for a second. Respect the waterfall that is your life. Actually, *enjoy* the waterfall that is your life. That's what it's there for. To enjoy. And to help others do the same. Go up when the water goes up and down when the water goes down.

For the longest time I thought I could force "balance" by adhering strictly to my carefully laid out lists and agendas. Lately, I'm finding that more often than not, I achieve balance in *spite* of my plans. My plans are actually kind of puny, no matter how much thought I put into them. God's plans are grand. I still make a written plan (a to-do list in my daytimer) nearly every day of my life. But when it gets interrupted—by say, a sweet boy clinging to my knees begging me to stop moving—I've been trying to train myself to do just that—to stop moving. (It's on my list.) I pause, look up from my computer or the stove or the piano, and engage the person who is in front of me.

I look back on that day seventeen years ago when Tay-tay implored me to stop moving, and still feel a little sad. I had just dried off the swing-set after the rain. How did it not occur to me to take my little boy by the hand and walk with him back over to the play set taking a few minutes to push him on the swings? I didn't know then how important it all was, how I'd miss it all one day—the feel of his tiny shoulder blades in my palms, as I pushed him higher and higher; the sound of his cherubic voice hollering, "Do 'gin, Mommy, do 'gin!"; the way I could see how he was already learning to pull back on the chains and pump his chubby legs to go higher still. He was growing up so fast.

And now, he's pretty much *all* grown up. He is 20 now, and home from college for summer break. Just yesterday when he tapped politely (he is ever so courteous, that boy) on my office door while I was working, I had this overwhelming urge to invite him to the park with me so I could push him on the swings. Ah, but something told me it just wouldn't be the same. Ha!

So instead, we talked. I helped him with some scholarship stuff, and then he shared with me a couple of songs on YouTube by a new group he's into. Then we had lunch. I didn't get this story written yesterday. It was on my list. It had *three* stars next to it. That's how important I thought it was. *Three* stars! And still, it didn't get done yesterday.

Clearly though, it *did* get done—the story got written. You are reading it. Today, my waterfall has supported the writing of these words. It balances out if I let it. I'm learning to trust the flow, to differentiate between the times I'm procrastinating or being lazy and distracted for no good reason, and the times my deeper values are crying out to be honored, even if this causes my to-do list to be temporarily neglected. A whole lifetime of soul searching has been required of me in order to *define* those values, and this particular one is solid for me. It doesn't change even when the waterfall does: *People* are more important than *things*, in any given moment.

My "creativity" cup is overflowing all over my desk as I finish this story. I think it's time to pour a little something into another cup (the one that reminds me of my late Aunt Mickey—the funny one with the tongue handle) and do something goofy and playful.

I think I'll go to the park. And swing.

Cottonwood

The south end of Diamond Lake is my favorite. That's where all the lily pads are. One year, we arrived just after they had all bloomed, and the lake was transformed into a vast and fragrant, floating garden. I drifted out into the middle of the buoyant field of flowers on an inflatable raft, and lay there, practicing stillness as giant iridescent dragonflies—glistening magenta and periwinkle, teal and chartreuse—landed on my arms and legs, my belly, even my cheek. It felt good not to shoo them away. I was in *their* garden.

Lake life is different from beach life, though in many ways, the same. For me, it is the perfect blend of novel and familiar. I love our annual visits to the lake in Eastern Washington with Ted's family.

This year, the lotus blooms had already come and gone by the time we got there. Still, I was drawn to that end of the lake, this time not by the sight and scent of the floating garden, but by a *sound*, a lovely, unfamiliar sound. I had to investigate.

The lake is very tranquil in the mornings. Sometimes it is so much like glass that I'm reluctant to smudge it with my movement. I had taken a paddle board out to the middle of the small lake, then sat down lotus style, like the spent flowers, to admire my surroundings.

Nature in the Northwest is so rich and layered. Unlike the view from my deck at home on the Gulf—sea and sky—the vista here includes water and rock and low scrubby pine and towering evergreen and hill and mountain and cloud and sun and sky and heaven itself. It's magnificent. I took it all in, then closed my eyes, and that's when I heard it.

A brook made of breezes. The water was as still as a mirror, but the air above me shimmered and sighed. There was a kind of soft, tribal, percussiveness and a deep, solid *shhhhhh* in the air, like a very distant crowd applauding. And like the landscape, the sound was layered and nuanced, and again, magnificent.

I opened my eyes and looked around, searching for the source of this restful music, and my attention was drawn again to the south side of the lake. There on the shore, a tall trio of cottonwood trees stood rustling in the slight breeze. I didn't know they were cottonwoods at the time. I only knew they weren't palm trees or pines. And that their voice was sublime. I sat there listening for the longest time, watching the distant trees glimmer and shimmer.

When I got back to the cabin, I couldn't get the song out of my head. The next morning I had to get a closer look. I paddled over to the south end and sat down on my board about 50 yards from shore to take it all in, but the north wind that had kicked up quickly delivered me to the beach directly at the base of the trees, and I looked up.

What a frickin' mess! I studied the tallest of the trio and was shocked. How could a song so lovely emanate from something so disheveled and beat up? The tree was a wreck—an oddly beautiful wreck, but a wreck nonetheless. It looked half dead. It was totally without symmetry and all disorganized and tangled up in itself. It was a tall tree, taller even than the firs on either side. Up high, the foliage was dense and silvery green, but about mid-way down, the branches, instead of reaching up to the sky, began to droop tiredly toward the ground. And all over the tree, caught up in crooks of limbs, were hundreds of dead, leafless branches still hanging on, some dangling by mere twigs. More brittle castoffs littered the ground around the tree, and I noticed, low down at the base, a deep, angled divot hacked out of the trunk. Someone had tried to take it down. Without success.

No, this funky old tree was still standing. Still singing. You go, ugly ol' cottonwood!

Now, I swear I hadn't gone searching for a metaphor that day (or maybe I'm always searching for metaphors) but this BOM (Big Ole Mess) really intrigued me. I kept thinking about it, even after I got back home to my pretty palm and pine trees the following week. I did a little research.

Seems I'm not the only one who has been enchanted by the voice of the cottonwood. The famous Medicine Man, Black Elk, of the Oglala Sioux, observed, "... even in the slightest breeze you can hear the voice of the cottonwood tree; this we understand is its prayer to Wakan-Tanka, the Great Mystery, for not only men, but all things and all beings pray to Him continually in different ways." The tree symbolized honesty, humility and self-sacrifice to the Sioux, and their annual Sun Dance ritual is performed around the tree.

I was really curious about why the cottonwood's voice was so distinct. There were maybe a dozen species of trees on that little beach—alder, fir, pine, maple, to name a few—why didn't *they* serenade me? The short answer has to do with the shape of the leaves. The leaf stalk of the cottonwood is completely flat and flexible, causing the leaves to rustle in even the faintest whisper of a wind. The tree is utterly impressionable. I know someone just like that.

It is also absurdly precocious. (Again, I *get* that.) It is the fastest-growing tree in North America. Too fast for its own good, it seems, as the wood can be weak and brittle and prone to disease. But its fast growth makes it a great shade tree, even as a youngster. As a mature tree, the heartwood from the larger limbs or trunk will often start to rot, and the hollow branches break off, *providing access to the interior of the tree* for small animals—squirrels, opossums, bees—to live. Its brokenness makes it hospitable and accommodating. Hmmm.

And the voice. It was the voice that drew me in, and though I could see that the masses of quivering leaves created the restful rustling sound of the tree, I was still perplexed by the slight percussive undertones I had heard that morning—hollow, like distant bamboo wind chimes. And I learned that this was the sound of the tree struggling to survive.

It had been a very dry summer, and in an attempt to maintain the osmotic, or root pressure necessary to nourish the thirsty tree, the cells of the tree had begun to suck in too much air, causing them to burst and die. This sound has been recorded and magnified by bioacoustician Bernie Krause and is apparently a couple of octaves out of auditory range for humans. But I swear I heard it that morning. Very soft and acoustic, providing the backbeat to the susurrant leaves. The dying cells cause the tree to exude sap which draw more little creatures to the tree, creating a whole microhabitat for homeless birds and insects. The tree has to die a little, though, to do this. Hmmm.

And I'm not making this up—the tree is messy. Not always,

mind you, but once a year, the females of the species drop masses of white fluff all over the place—actually seedpod that looks like cotton (hence the name)—and also tacky bud capsules that stick like super glue to everything. It's not the most popular kid on the block in late May or early June. And then there are all those dead branches—tangled up in the tree, or dropped sloppily on the ground. Hmmm.

Clearly, the tree is "a little messed up," just like me. But its voice, oh, its voice. It still has so much to say. I love this messed up tree. And this messed up tree loves me, I think. Why else would it have wooed me that day, of all days, when I really needed to know some things about myself?

I had come to the lake that week discouraged and full of self-doubt. *What the hell am I thinking, writing a book? Why would anyone pay good money to read my musings? I'm kind of a mess, and no longer cute enough or young enough to pull it off. This is crazy. I'm too old, too flawed and too broken to be of any use to anyone.*

Too broken. And then I heard the tree song—bright and hopeful, *celebratory*—the sky was cheering, it seemed. The song filled the whole sky around me with pure tranquil joy. Einstein urged us to "Look deep into nature, and you will understand everything better." It's a good idea to listen as well.

Yes, gazing up at that bedraggled old cottonwood with its droopy, brittle branches, still clinging futilely to too much dead, useless stuff. I saw and heard in that tree the precocious, impressionable—yet hospitable and accommodating woman I have become. I can *tell* you about that, with *my* voice, and maybe you will want to turn my pages as you begin to hear the strains of your *own* sweet aria, your own essential melody. Maybe my song will help you to hear your song. And maybe, if I've sung mine well, with honesty and vulnerability, you will be brave and bless me with yours. Oh, that is the deepest desire of my heart. I need to hear your song. Sing it. Write it. Paint it. Play it. Sculpt it. Grow it. Whisper it to God alone if you're shy. But tell it.

Share your beautiful, broken, wise and weathered music. Your story. I need your story. And if, like mine, it is composed of shimmering heart-shaped leaves, and dead branches, and burrowing animals, and bugs and sap and rot and wind and sunshine and stars, I will know that you are true. And we all need more truth in our lives.

This is mine.

Stoker

Bears. Dehydration. The death of my soul. This is the short list. I could go on. But I only have time today for the short list—just a couple of the ways I could've perished. You wouldn't know it to see me now. I'm pretty settled in at this point. Ted and I may not have matching rocking chairs on the front porch yet, or lazy boy recliners in the family room, but we do enjoy a pair of tall and sturdy Adirondack chairs on the back deck.

We haven't always been such fuddy-duddies, Ted and I. We have been on some grand and perilous adventures over the years. (Did I mention bears, dehydration and the death of my soul?) We have also been to the Olive Garden there on Bayou Boulevard by the mall. That doesn't mean this story is without conflict. We could've starved to death that night.

It was back when the kids were in high school. We were killing time before Taylor's band performance at the football game. Ted and I had recently begun the sensible practice of sharing our main course when we'd go out to dinner together. Neither of us is picky, nor are we big eaters. Should be simple. You'd think.

The drama unfolded thusly:

(Fade in. Interior Olive Garden — Evening: Dinner rush at the restaurant. Ted and Sharla peruse menu for entrée to split.)

TED

So Sharla, what are you hungry for?

SHARLA

I dunno, everything looks good.

TED

Yeah, hard to decide.

Silence, while they get serious about the matter.

SHARLA

Did you see that scaloppini special—the one with the pork cutlet and portabella mushrooms? It says it's served with gorgonzola-filled tortelloni. What's a tortelloni? Maybe a super-sized tortellini?

TED

I don't know. But it does look good. What are you hungry for? *(again)*

Sharla scrutinizes menu for second option.

SHARLA

How about chicken? They've got a lemoncello-glazed chicken cutlet with your choice of pasta.

TED

Sounds good. Hmmm.

Silence. More silence.

SHARLA

Maybe we should ask.

TED

(Thinking real men don't ask for directions)

Good idea.

Small talk, small talk, small talk. Server returns for third time to take order.

SERVER

(politely)

So, have y'all made a decision?

SHARLA

(equally politely)

We've narrowed it down to the Lemoncello chicken or the Portabella pork cutlet. Which do you recommend?

SERVER

Oh, great choices. They are both really good. The chicken is a little sweet, with the lemoncello liqueur and all, and the pork is brand new on the menu, but customers really seem to love it.

SHARLA

Cool. Okay, can you give us a minute? And how 'bout one more of these?

(tapping the rim of my suddenly empty wine glass)

TED

So, what are you hungry for?

SHARLA

You know, it really doesn't matter to me. Whatever *you're*

hungry for.

TED

Whatever. You choose.

SHARLA

(thoughtful pause)

Let's try the chicken. Sounds interesting.

TED

(equally thoughtful pause)

Why don't we go for the pork?

I can't say in all honesty that I *consciously* manipulated my dinner that night. But, if I'd had my druthers, and I guess I did, I'd have gone for the pork. And I got the pork. So what the hell am I whining about?

I'm not. Not only did I choose my dinner, in a kind of roundabout way, I also chose my spouse. That Portabella pork cutlet was a couple of years ago. Spouse, a couple of decades ago. I'm exceedingly happy with both decisions.

(Rewind 23 years ago. Interior Seattle Home – Night)

TED

So, what would you like to do for Valentine's Day?

YOUNGER SHARLA

Oh, I dunno.

TED

No really. I'm off that day. How do you want to spend it?

YOUNGER SHARLA

Hmm. Wouldn't it be fun to stay downtown in that funky new hotel—what is it, the Monaco? Maybe have brunch at Sazarac? Wander around Pike's Place Market and stuff?

TED

Done.

YOUNGER SHARLA

And just one more thing …

TED

Sure. You name it.

YOUNGER SHARLA

I get to be *right* all day.

TED

Right?

YOUNGER SHARLA

Yes, right. 100% right all day long.

TED

(*A little irritated, and a little amused*)

Okey-dokey.

I think that this Valentine's Day gift nearly killed him, though he never complained. (I ask for jewelry and villas on the Riviera now, and he's fine with that.) Ted is a good man, and he is good to me. He treats me like I hung the moon—or other celestial body, of *his* choosing of course.

So the question remains. I found my Mister Right. When did he morph into Mr. Always Right? The truth is, he didn't. No morphing at all involved. Mister Right has always been Mr.

Always Right, and that is why (among other reasons) I chose him.

I feel safe with him, looked after, cared for. Never mind that I was 32 when we married and that I had lived quite successfully on my own since I was in my teens. Ted's confidence and adventurousness were a real turn on. Still are.

Once we were hiking alone in the Olympic Mountains. Really alone, or so we thought. We hadn't seen another homo sapiens in a day-and-a-half. We did, however, suddenly find ourselves in the company of a very large, very scary bear. Of course we were armed—with a small frying pan and a couple of plastic sporks (those nifty spoon/fork combos that inmates get). And, as luck would have it, we also had plenty of yummy bear treats in our backpacks strapped to our equally delicious bodies. Great.

"Fear not, trembling damsel in distress, for I am with you."

Okay, he didn't exactly say that, but that's exactly what he projected. And to be honest, it was pretty damn sexy. And we didn't get eaten up by a grizzly.

On a cross country hut-to-hut ski adventure deep in the Methow Valley in the North Cascades, we got hopelessly, perilously lost. *Lost*, ten of us. Darkness came on; we couldn't see the trail; we had run out of water; it was really cold; we were physically exhausted with our 30-pound backpacks; and after five hours of endless trudging, our hut was quickly becoming a series of distressing mirages. Dehydration sucks.

"Fear not, my frozen fräulein, for I am here."

And then he wasn't. After he assured us that he could build us a snow cave in a worst-case scenario, he ski-sprinted off, down the black trail, in search of more substantial shelter.

And then we were nine. Fortunately one of us was a paramedic, so we got over our distress at being abandoned by our illustrious leader. And we slogged on. And on. And on some more. *Lions and tigers and bears, oh my*! I swear I could hear them lurking in the snow banks on either side of us.

And then, another animal sound, almost human, howling in the distance. *Slog, slog, trudge, trudge.* Well, maybe it wasn't a *howl* exactly—more like a yell. A *yell?* Wolves and Abominable Snowmen don't yell, do they? A few more feet up the endless slope—and we all heard the same thing, a voice, not a Hound of the Baskervilles howl. A *voice* … "Over here. Come this way."

At the top of the little ridge we saw it, all lit up like a Thomas Kinkaid Christmas card. Our hut, our Ritz-Carlton, our Taj Mahal, windows opaque with steam, fire blazing—and my Ted, my Eagle Scout, my hero, smiling happily, stirring a pot of melted snow on the rickety old wood-burning stove.

That was the night he acquired the nickname, *Stoker*. He tended that fire all night long with such zeal and expertise that around midnight we ditched our sleeping bags. By about two, those sleeping in the loft were hanging their heads out their open windows. By dawn, none of us could remember *ever* having been cold and thirsty at any time in our entire lives, not to mention just nine hours before.

And Stoker was *right*. Had we taken the tempting trail-more-travelled the night before, we'd probably still be wandering aimlessly about in a blizzard. We'd be *really* tired and cold. Actually, I think, we'd be dead. I had never been happier to be married to Mr. Always Right.

Stoker is very often, dare I say, *usually* right. (Did I just write that?) And knowing that makes him especially adept and compelled to be in control. He realizes this about himself and actually has a sense of humor about it. He jokes that whenever the boys ask him for something, his immediate response is, "*No. Now what's your question?*" He named his little fishing boat, *Con-Troll Freak*.

Of course, all too often, the very qualities that draw us to our significant others can eventually make us want to stab them in the jugular with our sporks. But we don't. Because, if we're smart, we know that we have our *very own* set of dubious qualities that our friends, families, and co-workers are obliged to endure.

So, having refrained, all these years, from assaulting my beloved with plastic flatware or other handy makeshift weapons, I find that I am richly rewarded for my restraint. Stoker is forever my champion.

Whether I'm lost in a snowy wilderness or being threatened by bears—real, imagined, or metaphorical—Ted has my back. Always. *No matter what.*

I *know* this. That harrowing "no matter what" reared its monstrous head a few years ago. Bereavement and addiction and insanity converged, and I was lost. I wrote in my journal: *Grief is heavy and wears black and stays up all night. It turns off all the lights and sucks up all the air. It wants to stay even when you want it to go. It's messy and inconvenient and above all, it is dark. It cannot stand the light.*

I was in utter darkness.

Albert Schweitzer wrote: "In everyone's life, at some point, our inner fire goes out. It is then burst into flame by an encounter with another human being … Each of us has cause to think with deep gratitude of those who have lighted the flame within us."

And who better to have around when your inner fire goes out than an experienced Stoker? Mr. Always Right became Mr.-

Always-Right-There. *Always* right there with me, no matter how dismal, how terrifying, how bewildering it must have seemed to him, he was there, quietly, carefully, selflessly tending the ashes of my soul, looking for an ember.

And finding that tiny spark, he did what Stokers do. He stoked. He never hesitated, never blamed, never complained. He just did the next right thing. And the next one after that. And then again. Until the flicker became a flame. Until I was safe.

Should it have come as a surprise to me that Mr. Always Right would have an altruistic inclination for doing the next *right* thing? The aspect of his personality that likes to be in charge of the remote, the steering wheel, the entrée selection, and countless other trivialities—that exasperating tendency to vie for the last word, provide the ultimate solution, offer the sagest advice—that very personality trait, may well have saved my life. And I'm not talking bears here.

And yes, he is my hero. As corny, old-fashioned and maudlin as that sounds, I'll say it again: Mr. Always Right is my hero. I have no problem admitting that I was a damsel in distress, though my knight wore no shining armor; he rode no mighty steed.

He wielded no glittering sword to vanquish my captors. He sought no glory, reward, or even acknowledgment for his valor, and he will be embarrassed to read these words. My knight, my Stoker, my husband, took care of me when I had forgotten how to do it myself.

Plain and simple—and utterly heroic.

Creatures Great and Small and in My Head

. . . .

Wanted: SWF

am not an animal person. How many times have I said that in my day? (I looked around just now as I typed that to make sure my dog wasn't reading over my shoulder.) I realize that making such a statement may have cost me 70% of my readers— but wait, I think I'm being rehabilitated. Read on. You'll see— there *is* hope for me; I'll show you. Her name is Shuba.

See, I never was allowed a dog as a kid. That's my defense. As a pre-teen I *was* allowed a cat, a ferocious little kitten I named Angeltwilightnonotinkertumpin. Yes, I named her that. No wonder she ran away. Or maybe it had something to do with her perpetually empty food and water bowls. I dunno. But she disappeared one afternoon, never to return. I unconsciously searched for that cat for years, guilt-ridden over the neglect I had inflicted upon the cantankerous little beast. That was forty-five years ago, and I swear I think I saw her skulking across Via de Luna yesterday. I didn't go after her though. She probably wouldn't even recognize me. I've changed a little since I was eleven. Besides, she's probably still mad at me.

For nearly thirty years, the closest I ever came to having a pet of any kind was the warren of dust bunnies I kept under my bed and the litter of pet peeves I kept in my head. And that was fine with me. *Not* so much for my little boys though. And while I may not see myself *as an animal person*, I am so a kid person. Which eventually mandated that I become an animal person, however reluctantly.

I thought it best to ease into the role of pet owner gradually—since *I'm not an animal person*. Looking back, it seems that size determined my progression; from those tiny, fluffy dust motes, to an itty bitty Siamese fighting fish named Swimmy, to a trio of box turtles no bigger than quarters. Finally I made the grand leap to mammals—and adopted two adorable kittens, siblings, Crystal and Sarah. They really were a lot of fun and not too much work. After a couple of years of not starving them, I realized that maybe, just maybe, I had redeemed myself for my childhood negligence of Angeltwilightnonotinkertumpin.

So when my son Taylor, at eleven, started suggesting that maybe we needed a dog (actually he begged, sulked, argued, negotiated, cried, bargained and schemed), I didn't balk. I didn't run out to PetSmart and buy a beagle either, but I actually considered his request. Even though I still proudly proclaimed my *not an animal person-ness*, the mommy in me couldn't resist the quaint, wholesome idea of a "boy and his dog." A boy needs a dog. A dog needs a boy.

And I was sure there were plenty of just such lonely dogs pining away in some shelter, yearning for a Tay-Tay to love. We would rescue one! The *heroics* of such an endeavor appealed to me as well. Loved that word "rescue." Then when people asked me what kind of dog she was, I could proudly proclaim her to be a rescue dog—with my boy and me the super heroes who valiantly saved her from extermination.

Yes, we would dash right up to the Pensacola Humane Society there on Fairfield and save us a puppy dog. I imagined dozens of scraggly but hopeful puppies barking in perfect harmony with that Sarah McLachlan song, *In the Arms of an Angel*, behind bars, scrabbling excitedly over each other hoping to be noticed and liberated, by us. *Choose me! Choose me! Woof. Woof.*

Yay us. Only problem, I was soon to learn, was that *puppies*, as cute and friendly as they are, even the mutts (especially the mutts), don't really have to *try* to tug at the heartstrings of potential pet owners. Those wee bundles of fur with the big, clumsy paws—the *puppies*—generally get snatched up pretty quick. They're so dang cute that they could sulk in the corner of their cage with a cigarette and a beer, and still get adopted.

Our first visit to the shelter just about broke Tay-Tay's heart. Not a single solitary puppy in residence. And no, he absolutely would not be talked into the much *more* heroic option of choosing a sweet but mature *dog*. Me? I sort of liked that idea. I'd heard that having a puppy was like having a newborn, only without the bloody nipples and episiotomy.

But no, Mom. Only a puppy would do. So we were obliged to wait. The good folks at the shelter suggested we call every morning to see if any puppies had been dropped off and to hightail it over immediately if there had been.

It was weeks before we got a hit. Finally, a puppy! A Single White Female, waited, languishing, surely for us. But we were advised to hurry. I snatched Taylor off the school bus, shoved him in the car, and we sped off to save the day, red capes flapping in the wind.

We arrived, somehow breathless, as though we really *had* flown across town using our super powers. We barged into the foyer of the shelter triumphantly like a couple of cartoon Mighty Mice—*Here we come to save the DAYYY!*—and demanded to see our puppy. The volunteer, the same one we had spoken to just minutes earlier, stuttered a little when she noted Taylor's sweet and eager face. "I'm s-s-sooo s-s-sorry, but there's already someone out there with her. He just got here, maybe three minutes ago."

I'm not sure how, but it seemed that Taylor, in the 23 minutes it took to get there had already fallen, helplessly, perhaps *tragically*, in love with this SWF puppy whom we had yet to meet. "Can't we just see her?" He whined.

Oh hell, why not? The volunteer went ahead and led us out to the yard, where a man crouched in the grass, playing with what had to be the poster pup for canine cuteness. That dog was adorable. Pure white with a big ole black patch around her left eye. As I stood there coveting the little creature, Taylor took off running toward them. "Daddy," he yelled. "Let me hold her!"

Ted stood and turned, white fur all over his slacks. And we both knew. We were now animal people—dog people, specifically. I had called Ted at work as we crossed the bridge into town to warn him that that this might be our fate today. For Ted to have gotten there before we did, he must have dropped everything and used *his* super hero powers to fly across town. He just doesn't miss a beat, that man. But he did miss a little work.

We spent two hours and two hundred dollars at PetSmart. We didn't have so much as a doggy dish at home. Taylor cradled his little puppy in his arms as we browsed nearly every aisle of the huge store, consulting with his pet on every purchase.

"Do you like the pink collar or the red one? Do you want a Kong toy or a squeaky one? Is this doggy bed soft enough for you? Are you hungry? Do you want the salmon flavored kibble or the beef?" And on and on around the store till we had filled the cart with everything we needed to join the ranks of bona fide, card-carrying pet people.

I can't honestly say that I was head over heels in love with this cutie 24/7 from the moment we brought her home that day. Hell, I can't say I was head over heels in love with either of my *kids* 24/7 when I brought *them* home more than a decade earlier. But I *can* say that I never entertained thoughts of sending either the kids *or* the dog back.

No, Shuba, as she came to be called, (*Why?* I do not even pretend to know; it was Taylor's idea) was from the start, a natural member of our family. And she has taken her place with such eagerness, loyalty, and affection that, at this point, some eight years later, I cannot imagine our lives without her. I don't even want to go there in my mind.

But one night when she was about four, I had to go there. It was the night I knew I'd have to turn in my *not an animal person* card. Shuba woke us up whining piteously to go outside. She had not done that since she was a puppy. She bolted out the back door and was instantly, copiously, and noxiously ill all over the azaleas. *Sick as a dog.* I get it. I apologize for ever having claimed I was that sick.

And then it hit me. Our neighbors' gorgeous black lab puppy, Shuba's new buddy, Lucy, had died very abruptly just two days prior. She had contracted the very deadly and very contagious CPV2 (parvovirus) and died within hours of the sad diagnosis. The disease is spread mostly through feces, which as it would happen, seemed to be one of the best things about Lucy, as far as Shuba was concerned. The virus is about 90% fatal in puppies. Even though Shuba was not a puppy any more, we had kept her in since we heard the news. Were we too late?

I was nearly hysterical when I dialed the vet at 2:30 a.m. Just the thought of possibly losing Shuba had me sobbing. I had to let Ted do the talking. I was *way* more distraught than I had been when Swimmy refused to swim (only float), or when Ted stepped on little Barney the box turtle, or even when Sarah, our kitty, wandered off one midnight into the especially noisy coyote-infested woods, never to return.

I prayed hard for my dog. So did Ted. She did not have the virus. She did not die.

No, Shubadoo is alive and kickin', or actually lickin', right here at my feet. And I have to say—after all these years, ten to be exact—I admire the hell out of her. Really, she's such a cool friend to have. We have fun together. She makes me laugh. And I learn so much from her. Namely:

- It's okay to be fierce sometimes—even if it's only an act—to protect your peeps. Even if it means repeatedly skidding head first into the glass of the front door when the doorbell rings, hackles like porcupine quills, barking psychotically. Convincingly implying you'd like to rip the interloper's throat out. It's okay.

- Sometimes you gotta do stuff that scares the shit out of you, or makes you feel cranky. Baths are a necessary evil. Even if the terror of all that water—and the naked man in the shower with you that, come to think of it, looks an awful lot like your beloved master—causes you to wedge yourself under the bed, shaking like a maraca. It's okay. You'll do it anyway.

- If the gate is open and the sun is shining, make a run for it! Go outside. Every day, every chance you get. Who'd've thunk that jamming your snout, up to your eyeballs, into ghost crab holes in the dunes could be so much fun? It just never gets old. Nor does sprinting down the beach like your tail's on fire. So, you don't have your heart-rate monitor, or your fit-bit, or your I-phone to measure stuff. It's okay. Better than okay; it's actually fun. Fun is good.

- But sometimes being still is the best thing, maybe the only thing. Especially lying on the rug right beside a sick or grieving friend. You don't have to understand why she won't get out of bed again this morning to play with you, or why her face is red and snotty and swollen. That's her business. Your business is being there. Just being there. As long as it takes. And if you feel sad too, with her, that's okay, as well.

- Just because you're concerned, maybe a bit obsessively, about the welfare of your peeps, it doesn't make you the poster pup for CoDA. You are a pack animal, after all. You know that we can't do this alone. It's encoded in your DNA. It's understandable that you get a little nervous when there seem to be too many people at the house at once to take care of, to protect from UPS men. You do your best, and your best, even if it stresses you out a little, is good enough.

- It's not uncool to show your enthusiasm. If it makes you so happy that your whole body wags and you forget your manners and just have to hop up and bark joyfully *every time* he comes home from work *every single evening*, like he's a soldier coming back from a nine-month tour in Afghanistan, it's okay. No need to be coy when it comes to expressing appreciation and the joy of friendship. No need at all.

- It's just fine that you're not a puppy anymore. Puppies *are* adorable and entertaining and full of energy, and you *were* one cute little rascal back in the day, though you didn't know it. And it *was* so much stinkin' fun to rip the stuffing out of the bottom of that pretty Bergère chair in the living room, strewing big tufts of white wadding all over the place, causing your Person to wander, bewildered and furious throughout the house, trying to figure out where it all came from. That was fun, but this may be funner—or at least more satisfying—this more secure, thoughtful way of doing things. Plus, you're not in trouble all the time.

- Yesterday and tomorrow? Not concepts you can relate to. Even *today* is a bigger chunk than you're inclined to gnaw on. *Now* is where you live, and that makes you very forgiving, appreciative and fun to be around. Remember that time He got so mad He threw a paint brush at you? *No. No, you don't.* Remember when your People had to use bolt cutters to remove the fish hook from your upper lip? No. Not really. Remember when your water bowl was empty, when you needed to go outside and no one was home to open the door, when they *all* left with those big boxes they call suitcases and didn't take you with? No, none of this really rings a bell. It doesn't matter. This does. This *now*, on the blanket at Her feet.

Yes, Shuba is a good little teacher, and she does it the way all the best instructors do—by example. By being herself. She only knows how to be a dog, and I have never once caught her trying to be a dolphin or a pelican.

Yesterday, on our walk, we encountered a surfer on the beach with his gorgeous young boxweiler—on a leash, thankfully.

(Someone had "forgotten" Shuba's leash; the beach is mostly deserted this time of year.) Shuba trotted right over to say hello; it's just the neighborly thing to do. Shuba loves *all* dogs and *all* people—with the singular exception of the UPS man.

The boxweiler's owner tightened his grip on her leash and gave us the go ahead. A few feet short of the brawny young dog, let's call her Brunhilda, Shuba crouched low in the sand, and proceeded very warily. But proceed, she did. Her social instinct is very strong, even over-riding her common sense at times. I know someone just like that.

Still, Shuba approached the dog respectfully, inching ever closer till they met, and they began that icky little butt sniffing dance dogs do, and Shuba was sooo happy. *A new friend. A new friend. Yay-yay-yay!*

Brunhilda, maybe not so thrilled. She endured Shuba's exuberant welcome for a few seconds, then started to get a little growly. Well, okay then. And we were on our merry way.

I extended our walk much further down the beach in hopes of avoiding another encounter with Shuba's new "friend," but they were still there when we returned. And Shuba, having already "forgotten" the cool reception she had received a few minutes earlier, again approached the burly dog. Her owner, apparently working on socialization with her, invited us over, leash triple wrapped around his hand.

Good thing too. As it turns out, Brunhilda was feeling a little cranky about these forced encounters and was in no mood for more butt sniffing. She lunged, like a wolf on Bambi, and knocked Shuba sideways into the sand. Her owner yanked back on the leash before Brunhilda could eat Shuba's head, and Shuba yelped once and ran away into the dunes.

Where she stayed. And wouldn't come out.

For about two-and-a-half minutes.

Then she bounded playfully through the sea-oats and raced happily toward the house.

How much fun is this? I could hear her thinking as she charged down the beach, the strong west wind peeling her lips back into a goofy smile. *But what about that dog that wanted to eat your face a minute ago?* I countered.

She looked at me—in that quizzical, head-cocked way that dogs do. And took off again. *How much fun is* this?

Her animal person followed happily behind.

Fido

Itry so hard, really I do, not to get ruffled by the minor irritations in my life. I remember when that clever little book, *Don't Sweat the Small Stuff, and It's All Small Stuff*, came out in the late 1990s. I had just ended a 17-year career as a flight attendant to begin a lifetime vocation as a wife and mommy. The boys were toddlers; Ted was traveling abroad for work; I was frazzled.

I remember being in the Elliott Bay Book Company on 10th Avenue in Seattle, with both sticky boys in tow and reading the sub-title: *Simple Ways to Keep the Little Things from Taking Over Your Life*. And I had to laugh. The *little things*, these little creatures wriggling and whining there in the big blue double stroller hadn't merely taken over my life; they *were* my life. And I was overwhelmed. Everything irritated me.

So I bought the book, with the sudden realization that if I was going to survive this transition, and more importantly, if my boys were going to live to tell the tale of their childhoods, I was gonna have to prioritize my pet peeves, only keep the really cutesy ones, muzzle the most vexatious ones, and send the rest to obedience training.

Actually, I'd like to be rid of them all. They seem to be a solid waste of emotion and energy. They bum me out. The term itself, "pet peeve," could *be* one of mine if I were allowed to have one. *How much is that tantrum in the window?* A *peeve*, an irritation that you coddle like a cherished animal, really seems stupid. If I'm irked about something, isn't it rather self-destructive of me to toss the Frisbee for it on the beach and reward it with yummy doggy treats?

But that's what we do. We nurture our gripes, play games with them, build up elaborate defenses of them and yak about them incessantly. We take them to the vet to get their shots and to the groomer for a pedicure. Go figure.

And we wonder why our dentist prescribes a night guard, why the bottom of the bottle comes so fast, why our blood pressure scales Everest every time we drive in traffic. These things *get* to us. They stress us out. These fuzzy little pets of ours have teeth. Sharp ones. They bite.

Of course, I have more than one pet peeve. But I've trained a lot of them to behave. Most of my little creatures are common mutts. Little annoyances that most everyone admits to having: poor grammar, rude drivers, tardiness. But some of my little pets have pedigrees; they have cost me a lot to maintain. I have so much invested in them. They yip and yap there on my lap, and I let them carry on because it is easier to indulge them than it is to muzzle them.

For example, it makes me crazy when I hear someone talking "authoritatively" about something they know nothing about. This happens a lot in a gym, where I spend a good portion of my work week. I also see it on TV and on Facebook. And, alas, it often happens at home. And the really sad part is that *I*, as often as not, am the one spouting nonsense.

This has always been an issue for me. And the Universe does

know how to take me down a notch. Back when I was a flight attendant, I took great pleasure in Christmas shopping around the world for my family and friends. I loved buying gifts for people, and I put a lot of creative thought and energy into the process. I still do. I want to find the perfect gift for you. It's a great perk of being my friend.

Back then the whole world was my shopping mall. Literally. I bought antique brass milk cans in India, delicate Venetian lace gloves in Italy, Waterford glass tumblers in Ireland, pretty pink Mikimoto pearls in Japan. I brought back new Beaujolais from France, macadamia nut brittle from Hawaii, and creamy chocolate truffles from Switzerland.

The chocolate was for my sister. She loves chocolate. I bought the candy at the duty-free shop in Zurich for about 20 Swiss francs, which seemed like an awful lot of money for a dozen bonbons. But my savvy, much-worldlier-than-I flying partner explained to me that these were no ordinary confections. These were special. These were Swiss *truffles*. And she went on to explain to me the genesis and evolution of this dusty little brown orb of gastronomic exquisiteness.

Who would have guessed that these sweet, delectable chocolate treats had been rooted out from under the dirt in some European forest by horny little pigs called truffle hogs? Yes, I went on to explain, these clever little porkers have been trained to hunt on a leash for the tasty little tubers buried deep under the ground. Apparently the smell of the truffles is thought to be similar to the scent of the male pig's sex hormones. No wonder they were so expensive.

That was my story. And sadly, I was sticking to it, there around the Christmas tree that Christmas Eve at my sister's in 1981.

No one thought to correct me, though I noticed that no one was in a big hurry for dessert that night. It was a couple of years later when I noticed an egg dish with truffles on a room service menu at the InterContinental Hotel in Hong Kong, that I began to question the whole truffle story. As sophisticated as I fancied my palate to be after five whole years traveling the world, I still couldn't reconcile the culinary pairing of scrambled eggs with chocolate.

To this day, I do not cook with or serve truffles—neither the fungi nor the confection. But I continue to mess up words and concepts occasionally and to speak animatedly of things I know nothing about—especially if I want to impress you.

I remember once when I was in my late 20s, I met an impossibly handsome, worldly young doctor at a sushi bar in Manhattan Beach. Conversation in the group drifted to politics—not my strong suit, then or now—but I was delighted when he asked me if I subscribed to *Harper's*. Why I just *happen* to have the most recent issue on my coffee table—the one with Carol Alt on the cover, and a list of America's 10 most eligible men (of which, OJ Simpson was one, ha!). It was at least a decade before I realized that the venerable *Harper's Magazine* wasn't quite the same as the *Harper's Bazaar Magazine*, I liked to read on my jumpseat at work.

Life coach Sharon Lamm coined the phrase, *You spot it, you got it*. And as much as I hate that little bit of insight, I have to admit that so many of the things I'm critical of in others, I struggle with myself.

So, these days when I hear someone say something like, "I'm so hungry I could eat myself into Bolivia," I'm more likely to be amused than peeved. *Bienvenidos a La Paz!* There but by the grace of God go I. And when people just can't get their prepositions and verbs to get along with their pronouns, I refrain from correcting their grammar. It's none of my business unless I'm their mommy or their teacher.

Those grammar and language usage peeves are the easiest for me to defang. Especially when looked at in such a way that makes me laugh—usually, at myself. The more I rant about the use of the non-words: *nuculer, jewlery,* and *realator,* the cleverer I hope to appear. I'm such a smarty pants. I like to appear smarter or more sophisticated than the next guy. It's not one of my better qualities.

Still, there are whole other categories of peeves that I find harder to relinquish. Usually, these involve courteousy, or lack of it—or what I perceive it to be. These encompass myriad social situations—on the road, in the grocery store, at parties, alas, at home. Anywhere I have to interact with other humans. These are harder to dismiss because, of course, I'm *right*. There is a rock-solid moral imperative embedded in my indignation, and I'm only making you a *better person* by pointing out the errors of your ways.

Yeah, right. My 80-year-old mother-in-law's character is greatly improved by being told the *correct* way to fold a towel. My husband is a *better man* when he places his keys and wallet *in the basket* on the counter after work instead of on the counter. My boys are much more intelligent and humane when they make their beds in the morning.

Or maybe they are all fine just the way they are. My mother-in-law has been folding towels lengthwise since way before I was born, with no ill effects that I can see. Ted's keys and wallet take up the same amount of space in a basket as they do on the counter. And, I have to admit, Taylor had a point when he complained that making his bed after he gets out of it seems like tying his shoes after he takes them off. He's just gonna have to untie them again to put them back on. Maybe they don't need me telling them how to function in this world. If that's the case, and I'm suspecting it is, then it all comes back to me again, as it always does. I can let these things irritate me, or I can move onto something more productive than trying to control the inconsequential domestic behaviors of adults. This household category of pet peeves boils down simply to my *preferred* way of doing things. And though I try to defend my preferences by building them up to be more *functional* or *appropriate* for some *practical* reason, usually, a flip side can be argued.

Which leads me to my most irksome category of pet peeves— those manifesting in messiness or wastefulness. These are the ones I let stay up all night barking at shadows, peeing on the carpet and chewing up shoes. They are the ones that I lose sleep over. I can toss and turn in a tizzy over the dirty dishes putrefying in the sink or the gallon of milk left out all day.

Of course I can argue, with many sympathizers, that it is *wrong* to inconvenience others with your messes and that it is *wrong* to waste our resources. Therefore, it is *right* that I should be angry; it is *right* that you should be tidy and frugal. And I've spent so much time doing just that, that frankly, I'm exhausted. It's hard work getting grown-ups to behave.

I've been trying for decades to get my husband to see the light. But I can't even get him to see the panties—the bright red thong panties that I accidentally left wadded up on the bathroom counter in my rush to get to the airport for a flight to Sydney 25 years ago. No, they are not still there by the sink where I tossed them as I dashed out, but they *were* still there six days later when I got home. And even though *I* was the one who left the mess for someone else to clean up, I'm still all bent out of shape—*still*, nearly a quarter of a century later—that Ted didn't put them in the hamper, *where they belong*.

Where they belong! That has been my anguished battle cry for as long as I have cohabitated with other humans, especially the ones with the mismatched XY chromosomes. Why can't you just put it away? The dirty clothes hamper is right there, *Open!* The dishwasher is empty. The fridge is 18 inches to your left, *right there*—the big silver rectangle. It keeps stuff cold.

A place for everything and everything in its place. See, there's a *saying, an official saying* that supports my premise. I am *right*, dammit. It just makes sense to put stuff away.

Except when it doesn't. And for two of my three menfolk, it just doesn't. And it has taken me nearly 30 years to figure out why.

Ted's garage, at any given time, looks like Fred Sanford's front yard on crack. Myles' bedroom, on the tornado scale, is easily an EF4 aftermath. And yet, I can call Ted at work and ask him where the eight-point socket for the wrench might be, and he'll direct me to within three centimeters of it on his workbench. Because he remembers seeing it there. Two Thursdays ago.

He has a freakishly accurate visual memory. He can remember the face of a person he glimpsed once at an airport in Warsaw in 1986. I, on the other hand, came within three feet of Lou Ferrigno at the airport—a.k.a. the Incredible Hulk—and didn't notice. But if Ted sees it or has seen it, he can recall it. Not only does he know where his keys, sunglasses, and wallet are at all times, he knows where mine are. *If* I've left them out.

Sharla Dawn Gorder

Which I try not to do because I'm the opposite. The more stuff I have to visually contend with in my surroundings, the more befuddled I become. Alas, the inside of my head is usually a jumble. When my environment is also, there is no homeostasis, and I become distraught. Since this is my reality, I've devised ingenious systems for storing stuff away, out of sight, out of my beleaguered mind. I need things tidy.

Jack Sprat, not so much. So, am I *right*? Me with my messy mind and immaculate counter tops? Is he *wrong*? With his incisive mind and littered workbench?

Whenever I have a conflict with a loved one, or even an *un*loved one, if I want to get along—and really, I do—I have to force myself to get out of my head, and into theirs—and try very hard to understand where they may be coming from. It's really not a lot of fun, and I wouldn't do it if I could just figure out how to get *all* people to see *all* things my way at *all* times. But disciplining myself to take a peek at others' perspectives really helps to keep my cutesy little pet peeves from becoming rabid monsters that will rip your throat out the next time you leave a fish head on the table.

Don't leave your fish head on the table, please. This really irritates me. I did not know that this was a pet peeve of mine until last month when Ted did, indeed, leave a fish head on the table on the deck downstairs. For three days. I have no idea where the rest of the mullet had gotten off to. And to be honest, I wasn't particularly interested in Ted's angle on the issue. I had to put my foot down on this one. Sometimes you just do.

But most times, you really don't. In fact, those people who *do*, the ones who are bothered by everything from slow restaurant service, to the improper use of who and whom, to dysfunctional turn signalers—those folks can really be a bummer to chum around with. Really. You know who you are. I mean, you know whom you are. Uh, damn, whatever.

Or maybe you don't. Maybe *I* don't! Maybe I wear my pet peeves like Paris Hilton's Chihuahua in her Hermes crocodile handbag. Or, maybe, and this is worse and far more likely; maybe I am unwittingly the peev-*er*, the one who does the actual peeve-*ing*.

The one who walks across the Publix parking lot at a scant five-degree angle forcing cars to inch along behind me 'til I finish my text. Or the one who says "no problem" instead of "you're welcome." Or the one (sorry hun), who leaves the top off the toothpaste even though we now buy the kind with the nifty hinged top that is *already attached* for God's sake. Maybe I'm *that* person.

Surely I am. So I owe it to everyone to extend a little grace when *they* inadvertently provoke my little mutt, and get Fido all worked up.

I had to muzzle him last Friday. And I'm glad I did. A dear, dear friend who actually truly loves me, noticed my less-than-chipper mood at the gym, and with a perky little wink said, "Smile, it can't be that bad." I *hate* it when people do that. I mean it *really* irks me. Who are they to tell my face what to do?

And, I confess, in that moment, I really wanted to sic my rabid mongrel on her right there at the Smith machine. Instead, I calmly explained to her that it *isn't* that bad, in fact, there's really nothing wrong at all, I've just got what they call a resting bitch face. I laughed. She laughed. Nobody got bit.

Atta boy, Fido. Lie down. Now who's a good boy?

Curious George Meets King Kong

Woke up with *monkey mind* this morning—howler monkeys on crack. Sweaty, smelly, shrieking monkeys, crashing through the tangle of my jungle brain, wreaking havoc. These were no curious little rascals accompanied by tall men in yellow hats. No, no, no. I could see their fierce and frantic faces, mouths agape—like Edvard Munch's *Screamer*. I could smell their fetid beast-breath, and feel the frenzy of their angry acrobatics.

Just go to your happy place, Sharla ... simply focus on your breath ... don't forget to pray ... get up and distract yourself ... go for a walk ... inhale, pray, move, distract, exhale, two, three, four ...

Ah, my monkeys. They do not always behave this badly. Sometimes they're even kind of cute—"fairly domesticated," like my Dad's. When he was in the hospital a few years back, and in the middle of a Haldol-induced hallucination, he gestured to the foot of his bed and asked my brother, "Jem, you see that monkey there?"

Jem looked around, alarmed, but Dad reassured him, "No need to worry, son, he's fairly domesticated."

Most of my monkeys these days *are* of the more manageable organ-grinder variety, with the dapper red vest and coordinating bellhop hat. But there are those days, even weeks, when these little guys wake up on the wrong side of the mangrove and invite some of their thug friends over to party.

It's no fun to wake up to.

The expression *monkey mind* is as old as the Buddha. Maybe older. According to an ancient Sanskrit metaphor, it would seem that my little mind-monkey has been up all night at the bar tossing back Jäger shots. To make matters worse, legend has it, he has also been stung by a scorpion. No wonder he's so pissed. And irrational. *Drunken monkey mind*, in agony.

What do you do with such a beast? Or more likely, a whole troop of them at 3:17 on a Monday morning when you *know* you have to take the bar exam at 8:00, perform brain surgery at noon, and save the life of a Romanian orphan at 4:00. You don't have time for this. *You have got* to get back to sleep!

But the night is so black, and your brain is so tender—still drenched in all of those yummy Theta brain waves—the dreamy ones that are so innocent and creative. But even the merest glimmer of consciousness sucks the juice right out of those sweet dreams, and the Big Bad Beta frequencies jump on your head like—well, like *monkeys*. This time, maniacal macaque monkeys.

Those are the monkeys that rile me the most because they are so damn senseless. They mess with you just for fun. What the hell does a monkey need with a lavender hair scrunchie? Perhaps I should explain.

It was 1992, and Ted and I were on our honeymoon, visiting the Sacred Monkey Forest outside Bali. And we had been warned. We were told, before we entered, not to accessorize. Jewelry, glasses, scarves—absolutely anything remotely blingy or colorful—had to go. I even, ever so reluctantly, removed my shiny new wedding rings.

There were clues even before we got to the gates that maybe this wasn't going to be the Indonesian version of a field trip to the San Diego Zoo. No, Padangtegal Village is a little more rustic than La Jolla. We were only a little curious about the big piles of rocks just outside the door of every shop in the village.

We saw the baby monkeys first, and they were adorable—which is another thing that pisses me off about this version of monkey mind. They draw you into their mischief with their itty bitty light-bulb shaped faces—two-thirds Margaret Keane *Big Eyes* and the rest, ears. They have perfect little baby fingers on their hands *and* feet. And those fuzzy little noggins. Damn, they're cute.

They distracted us from the should-have-been-disturbing entourage our little stroll through the forest necessitated. The *two* of us—happy little honeymooners in a foreign land with our *three* local escorts, brandishing big sticks. These guys flanked us, one on each side, the third following a few steps behind. Hmmm.

Still, the monkeys—hundreds of them—crowded the edges of the trail, scampering nimbly away from the lashing sticks of our protectors. We quickened our pace a little, nervously glancing left, right, ahead, behind—trying to keep them all in sight. It was impossible.

Should've looked *up* too. *WHOOOMP!* And twenty pounds of pungent primate plunged from the sky and onto my head. *Where the hell did he come from?* Someone should have told me that monkeys favor trees. Or maybe I knew that. Still.

I stumbled but didn't dare fall. Our protectors (some protectors they were) screamed Indonesian invective at the cheeky little bastard, and he seized my hair scrunchie and rebounded off of Ted's scapula, back into the tree from whence he came. If you're gonna have a heart attack on your honeymoon, there are far funner, sexier ways to make it happen.

I lunged for Ted, my *ultimate* protector, and he looked me over for evidence of injury, only he couldn't see my face. My giant permed mane of post-80s hair had been liberated from its elastic constraint during the attack, and Ted—in that lovely, nurturing gesture I fell in love with him over—brushed the hair from my face and kissed my head, the same one that had just been occupied by a monkey. Love that man.

Anyway, my question remains. What the hell does a monkey need a lavender hair scrunchie for?

Answer: He doesn't. He's just screwing with me because he can. Despite the stick-wielding guards and the rock-hurling shopkeepers, the monkey can still mess with me as long as I engage him in any way at all.

It is very hard to ignore a monkey sitting on your head. I'm sure you appreciate that. But it didn't have to go that far that day in the monkey forest. I could have taken a hint perhaps and gone to the beach instead. Ha!

It didn't have to go that far this morning in my mind either. The things I'm anxious about don't always need to be indulged. I don't have to enter the monkey forest in the first place. It is a neurological fact that the human brain is capable of but one thought at a time. *Yeah, right.* Tell me that when every vine in my jungle mind is possessed by screaming primates, crashing through the canopy of my consciousness, and eventually, inevitably onto my head.

Still, for me, understanding that only *one thought*—one monkey—can be featured at any given time, well, that's useful knowledge. Being aware that—at least on a neurological level—I actually have only *one* monkey to contend with at a time, can often calm me down just enough to remind me that I can *choose* another thought—a good, or even neutral thought. The trite *go to your happy place* mantra comes in handy only if I have not ventured too far within the gates of my anxious ruminations.

Instead, I can go to my Aunt Mickey's screened-in porch between the pool and the kitchen. I smell the chlorine and the biscuits and feel the rush of Florida heat on my face as I charge out the screen door and plunge full-belly-first into the bracing blue water.

Or I can go to Steamboat Springs Ski Resort, swishing down Sunshine Peak on Big Meadow Trail under blindingly blue skies, gulping down gallons of cold, unfiltered mountain air. Alone. Joyous in movement.

Or maybe I go to the soft, shifting floor of the Caribbean under 40 feet of sea, lying placidly on my tanks, peering up through dappled light and fish and fauna, breathing into my respirator. Only breathing.

This "brain-switch" has helped. And I've found that it's best to make that transition sooner than later. If I dally with the beasts, they multiply at an alarming rate, and no amount of happy place imagery can rescue me. It reminds me of my nephew's Doolittle shtick with the seagulls when he was little: We'd all be sitting on my sister's deck sipping wine, watching the sky turn magenta at dusk, when Justin would come bounding out of the house with a bag of bread.

"Watch me call the birds!" he'd holler and toss one crumb high into the air over the rail. A single fat white gull would swoop down from out of nowhere and scarf it up. *Aw. Cute.* But no more than four or five crusts later the pink sky would turn solid white with wings, as hundreds of greedy gulls descended from—*I don't even know where*—onto the deck for an impromptu rave.

Not so cute anymore. Remember that farmer who had his eyes pecked out in Alfred Hitchcock's *The Birds*? Well, I did. And I'd generally run for cover soon after the first few birds joined the party.

So why don't I do that with the monkeys? What keeps me there, wide awake in the dreary pre-dawn, bathing in banana juice, engaging with the little beasts despite my better judgment? And I *do* have better judgment than that. Why don't I use it?

There's a perfectly good explanation, and it is this: The monkeys, clearly, are a problem and since problems are meant to be solved—*I will figure this out*—once and for all. And *then* I'll be able to go back to sleep. Thomas Harris wrote, "Problem solving is hunting. It is savage pleasure and we are born to it." Once I get started, it's so hard to stop. My happy places quickly become nothing more than a distressing series of fleeting mirages, and I am desperate. And worse, I am *awake*, irrevocably *awake*! What now?

What next? A better question, perhaps, is what *before*? Is there anything I might do to effectively pre-empt the distress? My anxiety, of course, is not strictly episodic. There's an insidious tide of worry ebbing and flowing just beneath the surface of my consciousness so much of the time, bubbling up innocuously at odd moments, spewing like a severed carotid in others. I have always thought, *that's just the way it goes. It's the price I pay for being a sentient being.*

But do I really have to keep paying into that coffer? Might my resources be better allotted elsewhere? That's what I intended to find out one Saturday at a *Meditation for Dummies* workshop at my local yoga studio. Well, that's not exactly how it was billed (it was advertised as a free introduction to meditation), but that's kind of how I approached it.

Canadian Buddhist nun, Kelsang Rigden, entered the packed yoga studio quietly and sat in a folding chair at the front of the room. The chair was flanked by two TV tables adorned with azaleas, a small statue of the Buddha, a plastic bottle of water, and the venerable nun's iPhone. Her appearance was mannish— hair shorn close to her scalp, thick body swathed in voluminous burgundy robes. She had plain, unembellished facial features, but her voice was soft, soothing even.

She spoke quietly, and of *happiness* and of *choice*. As though one had anything to do with the other and that either had to do with meditation. Ah, I guess I already sensed as much. I was there seeking a little more *happiness*, a little less monkey mind, and I knew that I would have to *choose* some new behaviors and attitudes to get there. But knowing isn't the same as doing, is it? That's where the next part came in. She kept repeating a word I was more likely to hear from my piano teacher than a Canadian Buddhist nun: *practice*.

Meditation is a *practice*. And here's the very good news: There's no culminating Big Game on Sunday. The meditation *is* the big game, and the prevailing play is *choice*, over and over and over again—choosing to return to, in this case, the breath.

Now this was *not* good news for me. I had heard the directive to *focus on your breath* so many times in yoga classes that I almost felt angry. *What? This again? Is this all you've got?* I'd tried it and found that the monkeys *love* that tranquil space I'm trying to clear (like that path through the monkey forest) and they crowd the perimeters with aggressive intent, and how am I supposed to focus on my breath when there's a monkey on my head?

Still, I listened, feeling hopeful somehow, every time she mentioned *practice*. And this is very odd because I kinda sorta *hate* that word. It's one of those words, like *responsibility* or *discipline*, that develop a bad rap somewhere in a hazy childhood. Just hearing the word, *practice*, transported me back to Ms. Bienvenuto's tidy living room, her stern face looming over the piano while my fingers stuttered all over the keys for an interminable hour. I hadn't practiced and there was a recital coming up. The Big Game.

But fast-forward a few decades—last Christmas, in fact. My sweetie gave me an electric piano and I was delighted. I picked up a piece of music I had abandoned years and years ago and tried to play it. In fact, every day, several times a day, I sat down on the bench and put my fingers on the keyboard and tried to play it. It was a hard piece. And even though I believed it was beyond my skill level, I kept coming back to it.

There were two measures at the bottom of the fifth page that had me stymied—all those sixteenth notes and syncopated left-hand rhythms. No matter what I did, I could not coerce my right and left hands to do their jobs synchronously. I could play the left alone and the right alone, but never together. Still, I kept coming back to it. There was no big game to compel me, no recital to intimidate me, *just the music as I played it*. I kept returning to it. The title of the piece—*100 Years*—was appropriate as it seemed to be taking me about that long to learn it. I didn't care. I kept at it.

And then—it was a Sunday, several weeks later—I sat down and played the measures. Just played them. With both hands. Together. I actually cried. It felt so good to hear, to feel that music coming out of my hands, my soul.

You know where this is going, don't you? In the dozens and dozens of times I had returned to the piece, I had never "perfected" it. But playing it *imperfectly* over and over again was good enough. And even when I finally coordinated both hands, it wasn't flawless. But it was good. It was very good. Very good *enough*. I continued taking steps forward and backward on the piece, even on those two, specific measures until, suddenly, they became a part of my personal repertoire. Eventually, I was even able to stop judging my efforts as good or bad. And just play.

And later, the six measures on page eight called me to keep returning. I remembered that *repetition* yielded imperfect, yet great results before. And more importantly, it had begun to feel natural for me to just be there with the music. Well, some of the time. Not all of the time. Not even most of the time. But that was okay. Those glimmers, fleeting though they might have been, kept me returning to the music.

Returning to my breath. That was the only instruction given during the meditation. Sister Rigden didn't tell me what to do about the monkeys, or the itchy elbow, or the grocery list. She just suggested that I focus on the sensation, there specifically under my nostrils, of my breath, coming and going, going and coming. She insisted that the *returning to it*, after brief forays into the monkey forest, was not a *deviation* from the training, but the practice itself. I was meditating.

It turns out that my thought jaunts were not evidence, as I had always assumed, of my "failure" to meditate properly. No, they were a necessary part of the *practice*, and they probably always will be. So be it. It also turns out that my emotional default mode, that *insidious tide of worry ebbing and flowing just beneath the surface of my consciousness so much of the time*, can be reprogrammed with practice. Practice can create a new default mode over time. *That*, I believe, is where all of the touted health benefits of meditation—from relief from addiction, psoriasis, and constipation, to lowered blood pressure and reduced heart-attack risk—come into play. Sign me up.

I may always be plagued by anxiety that stuns me awake before dawn. But I'm trying, lately, not to let the monkeys scamper around after me all day long like I used to. Meditation helps. Writing helps. Playing my piano helps. Basically anything that requires me to *choose* a thought or activity that interrupts the rumination. And then I choose again. And again. I am practicing.

A wise friend recently encouraged me to trust that life is giving me exactly what I need practice in. This morning, it was monkey business. But I find, as the day progresses that it is also music and yoga and writing. I can leave the monkeys back in the Ubud Monkey Forest. They can have my lavender hair scrunchie. But they can't have me.

Ommm.

LOL

I learned to text from my niece, Jenna. Or should I say, *for* my niece, Jenna. She did this mean thing called growing up and moving away, and I needed to stay connected to her. Despite the tediousness of those early texts—no QWERTY keyboards or auto correct—and despite my innate terror and dread of all things technological, I learned to text for her. With one finger. Very slowly. With all the concentration and deliberation of a tightrope walker, I stuttered out my messages.

She was much quicker, of course. So when Jenna started introducing me to texting shorthand, I was delighted. And no abbreviation made it into our conversations more often than *LOL*. Jenna's texts were hilarious. Never in a slapstick or sophomoric way. No, she was wickedly clever and delightfully articulate. I remember the first time I "Laughed Out Loud" while staring at my phone. It was during a Bands on the Beach concert in the spring of 2007. It wasn't yet commonplace to see someone guffawing at a telephone. I glanced around to see if anyone had noticed. (I then self-consciously dropped my phone into the cup holder on my chair, which—surprise, surprise—my husband had just provisioned with a glass of wine. Ooops!)

To Laugh out Loud—I love to interact with people for whom LOL-ing comes naturally and frequently. It's one of the reasons

I married my husband. He loves to laugh, and he does so often. *Out Loud.* No silent amusement or quiet chuckles for him. If something strikes him as funny, he laughs. Big and sudden. Like a friendly explosion.

Me, I'm not so noisy about it. I wish I were. Usually, when something strikes me as funny, I *"L"*, yes, but rarely *"OL."* Unless, of course, I'm in a *group* of enthusiastic *"LOL-ers"*, why *then* of course, I'm *LOL'ing* right along with the crowd. Laughter is one of the few contagions I actually want to be infected with. And the Internet is my favorite breeding ground.

I'm not sure why *this* particular YouTube video is so hilarious to me; I don't even know why I clicked on it as I was scrolling through Facebook posts the other day. I'm usually drawn to posts that feature folks, not felines. But there was something about Simon, this little tuxedo cat, resolutely curled up on his side like a furry apostrophe, being dragged across the grass on a leash. At first I was inclined to feel sorry for the little guy, but after a few seconds, it was clear that Simon was quite comfortable, and ironically (for a cat), *doggedly* determined not to cooperate in any way with this particular mode of transport.

His colleague, a ginger tabby named Wash, was trotting alongside on a red halter leash, as if to offer encouragement. *C'mon Simon, it's really not so bad.* Simon wasn't buying it. No, not at all. He didn't so much as twitch a whisker as he was hauled torpidly through the grass. He did blink a couple of times, in that slow bored way that cats do—but he never lost his form.

Not even when Wash plopped down in the grass directly in front of him. Simon just slid right over the top of him, smooth as silk, and continued being dragged along, a perfect little parabola of fur. I have watched this video probably twenty times, and I

"*LOL*" every single time at the part when Simon glides right over Wash, just as apathetic as can be. I love this cat. I just do.

I'm sure there are lots of reasons this makes me laugh and why I'm not alone. This was Simon's debut appearance on YouTube, and the video has been viewed millions of times. It's funny every time I watch it, but *hilarious* when I watch *and* listen to it. The guy "walking" Simon and Wash, though you never see him, can be heard cracking up in the background. He is so tickled by the cat's insouciance. A little tag pops up in the bottom of the screen that reads—*Tyler's laugh is magical.* And it is.

Laughter is just the coolest thing, a true universal language. Of the thousands of languages and dialects on the planet, laughter sounds pretty much the same wherever you go. Babies, long before they are verbal, begin to laugh regularly by the time they are only twelve to sixteen weeks old. Even if they are born without sight or hearing they still have the ability to laugh. And babies laugh way more often than us stodgy old grown-ups. Like *20 times* more often, according to gelotologists—yes, there is a whole field of science devoted to the study of humor and laughter. I want that job.

The sound of Tyler laughing at Simon is indeed magical. But it's also the way people *look* when they laugh that makes it such a pleasurable experience. Another YouTube video, the most viewed non-music video in the history of the website, is just plain adorable. And flawlessly funny.

Charlie is the biggest-headed baby I have ever seen. His three-year-old brother is messing with him, daring him to bite his finger again. When Charlie chomps down, for real this time, the expression on his brother, Harry's, face is priceless. *What the???* ... *this really hurts.* "And it's still hurting," he wails.

But what really cracks me up, no matter how many times I watch the video, is when Charlie looks back at his screaming sibling, then at the camera, then cracks up *himself*, throwing his huge noggin' back with fiendish glee. It's hilarious. Charlie knew he was being funny, and he was loving every minute of it. People love being funny.

When I was in middle school, I had this gigantic crush on one of my older brothers' friends—actually, on all of them at one time or another—but this particular infatuation went on *forever*, or so it seemed. More than *two whole weeks* maybe, an eternity for my fledgling heart. His name was Grant Carlin, and I remember scribbling that name over and over in the spiral steno book I carried with me everywhere.

He was (and still is, some 45 years later) the funniest guy in town. I was (and still am, some 45 years later) Jem Sullivan's little sister, emphasis on the "little." My romance with Grant was limited to what I could imagine, which was surprisingly, a lot. Nothing carnal, mind you—I was twelve—but my fantasies were vivid, and involved lots and lots of laughter. After all, that was his specialty. I imagined us hand in hand on the beach, frolicking in the shore break, our laughter harmonizing with the elements. Or chuckling over an Orange Julius at the mall or maybe struggling to hold back the giggles from some inside joke we shared during Reverend Grabil's sermon on Sunday. Heady stuff.

That's what I imagined. Until reality broke the spell. He was far more fun to love from afar, I found. Up close and almost personal: I was sitting on my brother's white Challenger surfboard in the sand by the pier, *almost* having a conversation with Grant, trying to be charming and at least four years older, and I found that while he was indeed uproariously funny, *I wasn't.*

Not that I'd ever fancied myself a comedian. But I wasn't even mildly entertaining to him. In fact, I found that I was not even mildly *existent* to him. Big buzz kill. The romance was off.

That's when I first experienced the *reciprocal* importance of laughter. It helped form the basis for the criteria I unconsciously established for romantic relationships. I remember reading in one of those Cosmo quizzes that what women most wanted in a man was a sense of humor—*a guy that makes me laugh*. Yeah, I wanted that too, but I wanted more. I needed more. I needed to make *him* laugh, too.

Now, in conversation, I'm not remarkably funny. Witty with words, sometimes. Occasionally clever. But spontaneously funny in social situations? Very rarely. Still, I make my husband laugh. And I absolutely *adore* him for that. He's a gelotologist's dream subject. He's right up there with the babies—laughing 300-400 times a day. Maybe more.

Still, after a quarter of a century, we just crack each other up, even during the hard stuff—the really serious stuff. Yesterday, we went together to visit with my parents at their assisted-living facility. Mom has been on hospice care for so long, and it's just not a jolly place to be right now. I sometimes even feel a little ill as I cross the courtyard on my way to Mom's bedside. It's just sad.

Making small talk, to distract me as we rode up in the elevator, Ted remarked that he was finally starting to get used to his new glasses. He has never worn glasses before, and we had been talking about the way it takes the brain a while to adapt—*cortical reorganization*, it's called. Ted was quite proud of his cortex's expeditious adaptation. Me, not so much. I told him that in his case, it was like rearranging the deck chairs on the Titanic.

He roared—that happy explosion that is his laugh—and we

left the elevator humming the chorus of *Nearer My God to Thee.*

We *get* each other, and there is something so affirming, so *happy* about that. I don't have to be happy to laugh, but laughing has the inevitable side effect of making me feel happy, if only for a minute. It's worth it.

Which is why Simon, and Charlie, and Ted, are all such important guys in my life this week. Simon helps me laugh about myself; how often do I feel like I'm being dragged apathetically through life? Charlie helps me laugh about others; people just sometimes can't resist messing with you. And Ted helps me laugh about life; sometimes it just sucks, it does, but it's still an adventure worth celebrating if I can only remember to use more than my right index finger when *LOL-ing.*

....

Raised in a
Barn - by
Wolves

Myles and the Tapir

Myles was little, about four. An age I've always loved—still pudgy and round like a toddler, but becoming a real, little man, with humor and opinions and itches in places he shouldn't scratch in public.

But like I said, he was four. And male. And born to scratch his nether regions. I, being the mom, and not four and not male, did my best to discourage the behavior, gently explaining that he'd need to keep his paws out of his tidy whiteys until he got home from pre-school.

Well, by the time I picked him up that day, he was clawing so ferociously at his hiney that nothing short of a straight-jacket could have prevented him from getting at that itch. He wriggled and writhed and whined all the way home.

I, being the mom, and not four and not male, had decided that it must be a hygiene issue, and promptly plopped him in the bathtub for a good de-lousing. He was happy enough for a while. A short while. Within minutes of toweling him off and getting some fresh britches on him, he was back to digging around back there again.

What to do, what to do? He wasn't enjoying this any more than I was, that's for sure, and I, being the mom (you know the rest) had really not had a lot of experience with itchy bottoms to draw upon. So I called the pediatrician. The nurse got on the line, and this is what she said:

"It sounds like he might have pinworms."

"Pinworms?" said I casually, trying not to sound totally grossed out.

"Yes, pinworms, it's not uncommon in small children, and once diagnosed, can easily be treated with a single dose of a medication called Mebendazole."

"Great. So I'll bring him in in the morning."

"Yep. We can get him in around 10:00 tomorrow, but you need to do some investigating tonight."

Investigating? This was getting weird.

Apparently pinworms are stealthy little critters that can abide quite happily in the large intestine of unsuspecting preschoolers for months. When the female pinworms are in a family way, they migrate down the colon and lay a few thousand eggs around the anus, causing intense itching and irritation of their host's hiney.

My mission, should I choose to accept it, was to capture a few of the offenders and deliver them to the pediatrician for closer inspection. All I would need was a flashlight and some scotch tape. I was instructed to wait until Myles had been asleep for a couple of hours, go in with a flashlight, roll him over and carefully search his bottom for signs of breeding. I could then collect the eggs on a strip of scotch tape and preserve them in a zip-lock till morning.

Yeah right. I was gonna go in, flip him over, de-pants him, shine bright lights in his butt, tape his anus, and furtively sneak out without being noticed. *I don't think so.* He had never been a sound sleeper to begin with, and it seemed to me that the aforementioned scenario would not be pleasant to wake up to.

That's the stuff future psychotherapy sessions are made of.

I knew I'd have to talk to him about my plan, but I wasn't quite sure how to explain it all without worrying him. Perhaps a visual aid would be helpful. Encyclopedia Britannica to the rescue. I grabbed Volume 11, bundled Myles up in my lap and began my explanation.

There was one little problem. I had confused my parasites and grabbed the "T" volume—for tapeworm, instead of the "P" volume—for pinworm. I wasn't aware of my error and opened the book up to page 554, where, sure enough, was a grainy little picture of a worm.

It was all going well enough until I got to the part about the mommy parasite coming out of his bottom in the middle of the night to lay eggs. He looked at the picture, looked at me, looked back at the picture and swallowed hard. He didn't cry, but his little voice quivered as he solemnly asked, "Will it hurt, Mommy?"

"No, punkin. Maybe just itch a little."

"Okay, Mommy," was all he said.

Well, it just so happens that on the adjacent page of my open encyclopedia was another picture. There, on page 555, was a photograph of a tapir.

Now for those of you not familiar with herbivorous mammals of Southeast Asia, let me explain. I had just, in effect, told my four-year-old that a 400-pound rhinoceros-like animal was going to squeeze out of his rectum in the night, lay several thousand eggs and die. But not to worry—*it wouldn't hurt a bit. Maybe just itch a little.*

And "Okay, Mommy," was his tremulous reply.

He looked up at me with those big blue eyes, and said, "Okay Mommy."

And this is how I came to understand the biblical adage concerning the "faith of a child." Myles trusted me. Despite what must have seemed to him like overwhelming odds, he trusted me to keep him safe. To tell him the truth, to be his champion. His ingenuous faith in me threw me for a loop that day. For the umpteenth time since I began this mommy adventure, I was challenged and humbled by the gravity of my vocation.

How could I possibly be the person he believed me to be, needed me to be, deserved me to be? How, when I don't even believe in *myself* so much of the time, could I be a person he could *always* believe in? The challenge of a lifetime is taking me a lifetime to meet. And it got a lot harder before it got easier. The teenage years were as perplexing to me as those toddler years must have been for him.

The issues changed. *Oh, how they changed*. It suddenly seemed that he wouldn't trust me to sharpen his pencil, let alone extract a large mammal from his bottom. I knew I was in for a demotion. No longer the hero, the Koolaid Mom, the one with all the answers. His practical perception of me *had* to change in order to accommodate his budding autonomy. But his heart knew me, and my heart knew him.

Underneath that shaggy, baggy boy with blackheads on his forehead and scabs on his shins, was a child who needed me to be his soft place to fall, his protector, his advocate. And even when he thought he didn't believe in me, I believed in him. When he needed his space, I cleared it for him. When he couldn't stand me, I stood by him.

And when his bottom itched, he could go ask his dad.

Not Tonight, I Have a Headache
or
The Truth about the Truth and Other Lies

Tay-tay was five. He stood in the doorway, redolent of chlorine, with his Ducky Duddle towel wrapped around his tummy.

"Go in your room and put your jammies on, Punkin."

"But Mommy, my toe hurts," he whined.

"Your toe? What happened to your toe?" He had been frolicking happily in the pool thirty seconds earlier. I walked over and inspected the offending toe and found no gore, no dangling toenail, no flesh-eating fungus.

"Your toe looks fine to me, Darlin'. Now go get dressed."

"But Mommy, I can't walk."

Here we go again.

"You can't walk, huh? You really can't walk?'

"No, Mommy. I really can't."

"Taylor, look at me?" I demanded. "Are you telling the truth? We've talked a lot lately about how important it is to tell the truth. Now look at me and tell me the truth."

"I can't walk." Quietly, this time, without moving his lips. He did this whenever he asked for something he knew he couldn't have, or whenever he was lying. I guess he figured if no one actually saw his mouth move, he hadn't *officially* said what he really shouldn't have said. Five-year-old logic. Go figure.

Taylor lifted the worrisome appendage and gingerly placed it atop his "good" foot. I stormed back to the sofa and picked up a book to read to my other son.

"Mommy!" Wailing now. "It hurts!"

"Taylor James, you get to your room this minute and put on your pajamas!"

I've had enough.

"I can't walk."

I've had more than enough.

"Taylor," I hissed, "You will go to your room and put on your pajamas if you have to crawl. If you have to slither on your belly like a snake, you will do it!"

With that, I furiously began reading to Myles—something about a moose and a muffin—while Taylor stood on one foot in the doorway, loudly bemoaning his disability.

I read louder. That moose had never led such an impassioned life. Taylor moaned harder. I picked up another book. Taylor stood his ground, as soggy as it was, as precarious as he was. And I stood mine.

Finally, I hear the *fap-fap* of tiny wet feet, or *foot*, on the tile behind me. I glanced back to see Taylor hopping solidly toward his room.

Seconds later he emerged dressed, still hopping—on the other foot now—to join Myles and me on the couch. We were still ignoring him.

A couple of books later, I announced that it was time for dessert. Taylor was up and at 'em—racing to the snack cupboard before he remembered his affliction. I gave him the evil eye, to which he simply responded, "It doesn't hurt anymore."

Argh! What's a mom to do?

I have a problem with duplicity, at least in part because I find *myself* so capable of it in certain situations. I have to constantly be aware of my tendency to hyperbolize. But Taylor, at five, had no such compunction. He could "fib" with such casual aplomb that I would often find myself swayed, despite his chocolate mustache and sticky fingers. My older child was just the opposite. Myles would not only tell you about the cherry tree, he'd march right out and plant a whole orchard of replacement trees.

To this day, Myles will tell the truth, even when it hurts. When he was about seven, he and his best friend Brian were horsing around on the couch.

Suddenly Brian erupts in shrieks of agony.

"Ms. Sharla, Ms. Sharla! Myles kicked me! He kicked me in the head!"

Brian staggers into my office, wailing. Myles tags along behind murmuring, "I'm sorry, Brian, I'm really, really sorry, I'm so sorry Brian ..."

I inspect his noggin', rig up an ice pack and attempt to get to the bottom of the altercation. Brian is still sobbing but has amended his original accusation, "Myles kicked me. He kicked me in the head! But it was an *accident!*"

After we all agree that there was no malice intended, Brian is free to recover, and they resume their play.

A while later, while playing the *whack-the-living-daylights-out-of-frisbees-with-a-baseball-bat-game*, a discussion of Brian's head trauma resumes. I walk outside just in time to hear Brian declare, with a certain amount of bravado, "Myles, you really kicked me good."

Before Myles can respond, I defend, "It was just an accident, though. He didn't do it on purpose."

Myles can stand it no longer. He has to fess up. "I may have done it on purpose. It really wasn't an accident."

"You did it *on purpose*? You kicked him in the head on purpose?" I yell.

"I might have."

"You might have? You might have hurt your best friend *on purpose?*" I wail.

"No, no, nooooo, Mom, I didn't *hurt* him on purpose. I *kicked* him on purpose. We were wrestling." And again, "I'm sorry Brian, I'm so sorry, Brian."

With that, Myles apparently feels exonerated, and the matter is closed.

Confession is good for the soul, even the seven-year-old soul.

But what of the five-year-old soul? The child that would sell *his* (soul that is) to Lucifer himself for a KitKat. The one that I caught, up to his armpits in a five-pound bag of Chex Mix as he casually explained that Daddy said it was okay. The one that suffers sudden and mysterious debilitating afflictions when it's time to clean his room, get dressed, or brush his teeth. It makes me crazy. Where did he learn that fine art of malingering? Hmmm.

We had a babysitter. An enthusiastic barely-teen that we all enjoyed immensely. She was (and is) vivacious and smart and great with the boys. Her job was to watch the kids every Friday or Saturday night while Ted and I had "date night." The kids loved her, we loved her, and the arrangement was so agreeable to us all, that we invited her along on our annual vacation back west to visit with all the cousins for a month at Diamond Lake in Washington. To help with the boys, so Ted and I could relax a little.

Okay, so she was barely thirteen. Okay, so I'd never "parented" a tweenager before. Okay, so I was a little naive.

Our final dinner, at Olive Garden in downtown Spokane, sums it up.

Babysitter: I'm *staaarving*! I could eat this whole menu!

Me: Well, you'll have to choose. It all looks so good.

Babysitter: (after some deliberation) I'll have the Fettuccini Alfredo dinner and an order of French fries.

Me: Lizzy, that's a ton of food. You've already devoured a big basket of bread sticks and two cherry colas.

Babysitter: But Ms. Sharla, I'm *staaarving*!

Me: (Quoting my dad) Get what you want but want what you get.

Babysitter: That's what I want. I'll eat it all, Ms. Sharla, I *promise*.

Me: (Exasperated) Whatever.

Sometime later, maybe two Chiantis later for me, I did the responsible-adult table check. Tay-tay was slumped against Daddy in a pasta-induced stupor. Myles was busy making sea snakes with the paper from his drinking straw. Grandma Joyce was sopping up the last of her marinara sauce with a bread heel. Various and sundry aunts, uncles and cousins were finishing up their meals.

Babysitter was laughing uproariously with other teenage cousins—large, expensive, meal in front of her, barely touched.

Me: Lizzy! (No response; she can't hear me over her laughter.)
Me again: *Lizzy!*

Baby-sitter: (Looking up. Understanding.) Ms. Sharla, I think I have food poisoning.

Me: Oh yeah? Food poisoning, huh?

Babysitter: Can't eat another bite. I'm *staaarving* though! But I'm really sick.

Me: Sick? Really sick? (Standing up.) Lizzy, if you've got food poisoning, we'd better get to the hospital. It's just around the corner. Let's go.

Babysitter: (Gravely) It may pass. Let's wait a minute.

At this point, Grandma Joyce can stand it no more. Lizzy starts to defend her position, but Grandma silences her with an *if-you-say-another-word-I'll-have-to-hurt-you look*, and says simply, "Lizzy, stop talking."

This edict effectively silences us all. We pay for our meal and set off happily (healthily) through Riverfront Park back to the car.

Months later, Lizzy still stood by her fleeting intestinal crisis, and we still adored her. And Taylor, throughout his childhood, still suffered bouts of sudden paralysis, debilitating malaise, and Alzheimer's-like forgetfulness, whenever faced with something he'd rather not do. And I'd still fret over it.

I'd lose sleep over it. I'd toss and turn in bed lamenting the apparent moral degeneration of my baby. My husband, who loses sleep for one thing only, would reach tenderly for me in the night.

"Not tonight, I have a headache," I'd mumble.
Or do I?

Don't Take Your Dolphin to School

My boys are men now. Wow. They are grown. Yet, to my wonder and delight, they are *still* the babies, the toddlers, and the little kids they once were. Myles has always been *Myles*. Taylor, forever *Tay*. I wish I had known this when they were little. I would have worried about them less and enjoyed them more. I would have claimed a bit less credit and far less blame. I would have struggled with them less, adapted to them more.

I find it astonishing, now, that these virile young men—Myles 22, Taylor, 20—have simply grown into who they have always been—from birth, it seems. It reminds me of the Jack Johnson lyric to his daughter: "You remind me of you."

I kept a journal—I called it *Baby Daze*—chronicling their first couple of years of life. This wasn't the traditional "baby book" scrapbook listing milestones and achievements, with baby teeth and locks of hair taped to the pages. No, it was more of a *story* book. I told stories about them, detailed narratives of their antics, struggles, and passions. And like all good stories, character development was crucial.

I wrote pages and pages describing their characters—their personalities and dispositions—in real time as they became evident. I was in awe of them from the start. I still am. I reread

Baby Daze yesterday, cover to cover, and I don't know why it surprised me so much, but the adjectives I used to describe them *then* are the same I would use to describe them *now*.

I made a list taken directly from those pages. Myles, before the age of two was described by me as inquisitive, restless, social, fearless, honest, physical, determined, tender, impatient and compassionate. Taylor, I recognized to be contented, independent, dramatic, artistic, stubborn, smart, calm, opinionated and considerate. Their personalities were so different, so distinct.

I had never paid much attention to the personalities of babies until my niece, Jenna, was born. That was eight years before I myself would become a mom. Before then, I think I just figured that babies were kind of blank slates for us grownups to write our expectations and hopes on. But from Jenna's very first breath, she was anything but manipulable. She was just glorious—willful, determined and original from the get-go. My favorite photo of her was snapped in Hawaii, where she lived for the first year of her life. In this photo, she was only ten or eleven months old. She is sitting naked at the edge of the patio looking brazenly up at the camera, right arm thrust skyward, middle finger prominently displayed. So, *so* funny. So, so *Jenna*—rebellious, hilarious, confident, fearless. Exhausting. Wonderful. Jenna was my parenting tutorial.

Then, eight years later, along came my opportunity to parent my own "spirited" child. And though Myles wasn't quite as audacious as Jenna had been, he was, from the very start, a force to be reckoned with. The boy never stopped moving, relentlessly determined to get what he wanted when he wanted it and *how* he wanted it—no matter what. He had me wrapped around his sticky little fingers. I once attempted to scotch tape a broken banana together for him. On another occasion he talked me into reading fourteen books to him before bed. I had to draw the line though when he became enraged after I wiped his nose at the playground. "Put the boogers back, Mommy! Put them back!" he screamed.

Myles always seemed to know *what* he wanted and what he wanted to *do*, and it never occurred to him that he couldn't do it. Admittedly, this attitude in a two-year-old was exhausting for me as a parent. His skill set, at two, did not quite match his ambition, and he was often frustrated and demanding. I wrote, "I am reduced to tears by my two-year-old. I am *exalted* to tears by my two-year-old. I am a walking (stumbling) contradiction. I am a parent."

I added, "He, *too*, is a walking (running, skipping, galloping, hopping, charging) contradiction. In one moment he can impale your heart with his willfulness; in the next, he can melt it with his tenderness … Many days are battlegrounds. Everyone in our wake is a casualty. Then he comes and dries 'Mama's tears, Mama's tears,' or suddenly kisses Tay-tay on the head, or carefully covers my legs with the blanket, or quietly implores Ted on the phone, 'Daddy, home. Daddy home,' and my heartstrings play a symphony. Glorious music, the child inspires."

Yes, that bold, boisterous bull-dozer of a boy was, and is, at the same time tough and tender. He has always been deeply spiritual and empathetic and was very troubled by the whole Jesus on the cross image. When he was four, he told me, "they should have put the nails between his fingers and made him hold on, and then when he got tired, his mommy could help him down."

As a young man of 19, when I confided in him my worry over my mother's impending death, he told me, "Don't fear her fear, Mom. It creates a never-ending loop." Now, at 22, he can often be found on the lawn at Landis Green on the FSU campus playing his guitar, or meditating, or conversing with anyone who happens by. People go to him when they want to be heard. People need to be heard. Myles will listen.

Yes, that very same cluster of qualities I noticed in him as a baby—determination, focus, confidence and enthusiasm—when blended with attributes he displayed as a toddler—tenderness, curiosity, empathy and affability—served him well as a child, and later, helped keep him safe(ish) as a teenager. Today my boy is a college student studying physics, teaching yoga, climbing rocks and making music. He is now, as always, "a force to be reckoned with."

His brother, Taylor, is too, though in an entirely different way. Myles and Taylor are only 22 months apart in age, but light-years apart in temperament. Taylor was the textbook "easy baby." I read somewhere that easy babies make their parents feel as if they are doing a great job. Taylor was God's gift to a beleaguered mommy—a confidence builder, to be sure.

When Taylor was an infant, I wrote, "His disposition is tropical—warm and sunny with bright blue eyes dancing." At one year he was, "a white picket-fence baby, a babbling-brook baby, a four-part harmony baby, a cookies-and-milk baby, a window-box-full-of-tulips baby." At two, he was a "happy, animated, delicious bundle of two-ness." My previous experience on the parenting field—especially at the terrible-two-yard line—did little to prepare me for this contented creature. I was delighted. I wrote, "He is just a pleasure, every mother's fantasy baby. It is as though he really doesn't want to inconvenience anyone."

Taylor has *always* been uncannily self-soothing. With only

his thumb, or his stuffed dolphin toy, or his creative little brain, he could always find a way through his emotions without, as I mentioned earlier, being much of an inconvenience to others.

I'll never forget one of the rare times I saw Taylor furious. He was barely four, and I had just picked him up from pre-school. He came bounding into the house, tossed his little Pokémon backpack on the couch, unzipped it, dug around inside it, and began to wail. His beloved *Blossie*, his cherished stuffed dolphin, was not in there. Taylor had left him at school.

Despite Taylor's natural propensity for going with the flow, he, like all children, could be pretty stubborn when it came to certain things. Blossie was one of them. I had warned him not to take his dolphin to school (Ha, things you say to your kid when you're a Floridian). He was, and is, very particular about his stuff. I knew it would be hard for him to share Blossie, and the rule was that if you brought a toy to school, you would have to share it. I reminded him of this rule, but Taylor insisted on taking him anyway.

Now he was panicked. He begged me to go back to retrieve his dolphin, and when I refused, Taylor became enraged. He bawled louder, and flailed around the family room, flopping on the floor like a flounder, punching pillows and screaming at me that I was being a "mean, mean mommy." At first, I was shocked—Where had my "babbling-brook baby" gotten off to? I indulged his histrionics for a couple of minutes, then lost patience and screamed back at him.

"Taylor James Gorder, you listen to me!"

He looked up from the pillow he was pummeling, stunned—not used to being yelled at.

"I know you're mad, and I understand why. It's okay to feel

angry at me, but it is not okay to try to destroy things. And I'm tired of listening to you. You go to the back room right this minute! Do an angry dance, draw an angry picture, play an angry song! But you stay back there until you've gotten over yourself. Go! NOW!"

Now, this "back room" I had banished him to was hardly a dark torture chamber under the stairs. Oh, no. It was a big, sunny playroom outfitted with toys and books and board games and art supplies and musical instruments. He gave the cushion he was assaulting one last punch and stomped off down the hall toward the playroom. He slammed the door.

I could still hear him crying through the closed door, but only for a minute or so. Then all was quiet. Maybe too quiet? I resisted the temptation to go check on him, and started emptying the dishwasher.

About ten minutes later, the playroom door swung open, and Taylor came stomping out clutching a piece of paper. He marched right up to me, and without a word, shoved the drawing in my face. I backed up a little so I could see what he had drawn.

In dark purple marker he had sketched the same image a dozen times all over the page—a lopsided oval within a donut shape with tiny blobs of color splashing out from each individual picture.

Hmmm.

Now I had learned from my Aunt Mickey that you never ask a budding artist, "What is this?" It is much more respectful to ask them to *tell* you about their masterpiece instead.

So, I looked at the picture for a moment, then looked at Tay-Tay's red and snotty face. As kindly as I could, I said, "Wow, Buddy-roo, why don't you tell me about this picture."

His eyes narrowed as he looked up at me.

"Spitting mouths," he hissed.

Ha! Well, he had certainly told me! And without doing the very ugly thing he really wanted to do—twelve times, if I was interpreting his artwork correctly. He had expressed his fury quite well. With that done, he was free to go play with his "car-cars" until his brother got home from kindergarten.

He figured it out.

He still figures it out. Just a couple of years ago, he and his girlfriend had broken up, and he was so, so sad and confused. My heart broke for him. I knew of no cutesy parenting techniques for comforting this grieving teenager (the playroom had long been disassembled) so I just stayed close by and checked in on him in his room periodically. He slept a little, played his video games a little. Later in the afternoon I took him a grilled-cheese and some soup and found him sitting up in bed, drawing in his sketchpad. When I went back up to collect his dishes, he was asleep again, still clutching his pencil. I kissed him on the head and turned off the light.

The next morning, I emerged from my office to find him standing over the stove cooking an omelet. He looked up at me and smiled. I asked him how he was feeling. He said, "I think I'm okay, Mom. I just had to remind myself this morning that it won't always feel this way." He folded his omelet over onto a plate and sat down to breakfast.

Yes, those "easy babies" really do make parents feel like they're doing a good job. I feel good about myself when I'm with this boy. This man. He is 20 now, and any time he is home from school, I swear I can hear that babbling brook, trickling very quietly in the background. He is calm, and very considerate, creative and self-sufficient.

All that worry back then—Is Myles too boisterous, Taylor too reserved? Is Taylor too complacent, Myles too intense? Is Myles too reckless, Taylor not adventurous enough?

My poor kids. It must have been confusing for them.

It reminds me of the story of those three bears and the golden-haired girl in one of the 14 books that Myles roped me into reading to him that night so long ago. If I had only known, only realized the lovely, lovely truth. That my boys were never too hot, too cold, too big, too small, too soft, too firm.

They were, and they *are* like the baby bear's porridge. They are just right—lumps and all.

Triceratops and Tissues

It seems like yesterday, but it wasn't. It was February 22, 1998—the day Taylor declined to cuddle with me for the first time. He was two-and-a-half. I was heartbroken. Empathetic toddler that he was, however, he kindly offered me a triceratops instead. "Here Mommy, you can cuddle wi' he. He a baby."

That was the only entry in my journal that day 18 years ago, so I don't know how long I had to make do with a plastic dinosaur for my snuggling needs, but I do remember how much I appreciated his concern. He really didn't want to see me suffer. But he had places to go, people to see, a brother to torment. If he couldn't be the *baby* he knew I needed him to be, well, he wasn't gonna leave me high and dry. He'd give me one of his toys instead, his beloved triceratops. After all, "He a baby."

It always amazed me to see that even as toddlers, the boys already felt compassion and an innate tenderness that moved them to behave with kindness toward others. God had to have put that there. We didn't; we hadn't had time.

I remember once when Ted was helping Myles construct some sort of delightfully messy choo-choo train in the dining room out of pillows and blankets and tables and chairs. Ted looked wistfully at me and said, "Oh, I hope we don't ruin them." Right away, I knew what he meant. But I said, "Don't worry, we won't."

About then, Taylor, four months old, started wailing.

Now, from the day that Taylor was born, Myles' natural inclination had been to comfort his brother when he cried. "Hug, hug!" he'd holler and charge over to him, usually kissing him on the head as he enveloped him in his rough and tumble baby bear hug. So *urgent* was Myles' need to comfort Taylor that I often had to pull over in the car if Taylor was crying and Myles couldn't get to him, not so much to silence the baby, but to calm Myles down as he screamed at me, "Hug Tay-tay, Mommy, hug Tay-tay!"

But this time, as Taylor was hollering in his ExerSaucer in the sunroom, I got to him just in time to see Myles, not six inches from Taylor's unhappy face scolding, "Stop it Tay-tay. Stop it!" I was mortified. I was heartbroken. I was ashamed. He had learned this from *us*. Were we already *ruining them?* From the time he could communicate in any way, Myles' natural response to sadness had been to console. He wanted to *help* you if you were sad, not scold you.

Now, if you're *mad*, that's another story. I'll never forget the knock-down-drag-out fight we had over a diaper when he was less than two. He'd just gotten up, had his bottle, and was refusing to cooperate with a diaper change. It wasn't worth the battle initially; I let him play in his soggy shorts for an hour before I approached him again. He still wasn't willing to comply. We had breakfast, which led to further saturation of said diaper, followed immediately by copious and noxious soiling of both diaper and PJ's. As the mess began to migrate down his legs toward the carpet, I steeled myself to resolve the issue.

He struggled mightily as if defending his very life. He kicked and arched and screamed the anguished cry of an abused child, all the while splashing and thrashing about in unspeakably rank muck. I lost it. Rarely had I raised my voice with Myles, or anyone for that matter. But that morning I think I raised the *roof*. Myles was screaming; I was ranting; we were both rolling around on the floor like angry mud wrestlers—only this wasn't mud we were wallowing in. It was absurd. It took all the physical strength I possessed to get that diaper on him. I finally fastened the last tape, and he squirmed up off the floor and collapsed sobbing in my arms. We swayed there panting for the longest time.

The next "opportunity" to dry his tush came a couple of hours later. When I, ever so cautiously, presented him with my plan, he flagrantly refused to participate, running nimbly away from me and the proffered diaper. I, still embarrassed by the morning's strange skirmish, and weary in general, suddenly felt like sobbing, and that emotion must have registered on my face. Myles looked back at me, puzzled and concerned. Opportunist that I am, I further contorted my expression into a full-fledged, swollen-lower-lipped pout. After a moment's consideration, he marched over and retrieved a fresh diaper, handed it to me, and lay down in front of me, motionless and solemn.

He just couldn't stand to see me sad. *Mad*, well that's okay (maybe even a little fun), but not sad. A couple of weeks later, after a really rough night—Taylor and I burning with fevers and Ted out of town—Myles suddenly found himself the man of the house, at 23 months, and he behaved just as I suspect his daddy would have, had he been home.

After a hellacious night of drenching fevers, I dragged my sad, sick self into the sunroom with the boys, and collapsed, miserable, on the couch. It was a bleak, November day, made more wretched by my pounding head and aching limbs. When

I eventually summoned the energy to phone Ted in Germany, I was sobbing into the receiver before I'd even dialed the country code. Apparently alarmed by my sudden water works, Myles, fled the room immediately.

He was back in a flash, however, bearing a lone and wadded Kleenex, with which he proceeded to dab each tear, murmuring, "Mamma's tears. Mamma's tears," as he diligently dried each new droplet, patiently standing in front of me, dabbing, till his work was done. When I finally finished my phone conversation, and my cry, he said, low and serious, "Hug, hug," and did the same with such tenderness and love, I almost began to weep all over again. Instead, for *his* edification, I just smiled. Myles acknowledged, "Mommy happy." And with that, he toddled off to build a space ship to visit Santa Claus in New York.

He had been on this planet for less than two years. Fewer than 700 days. In that time, he had acquired only a few dozen words with which to express himself verbally. Yet he *knew*, he knew how to show compassion, how to offer kindness, how to do a good thing for someone who was suffering, for someone he loved.

And that just blew my mind. And they've just kept *on* blowing my mind like that ever since. For, despite my often-clumsy or even misguided attempts to be a "good parent" to my boys, I see so clearly, *we didn't ruin them*. Because at the core of everything we did for them, or *to* them—at the heart of all of that *parenting*—we were always deeply and reverently awed and impressed by who they were. Not even necessarily who they were *becoming*. But who they were in that moment; in that moment when my little boy devoutly dried my tears, or even in those (many) moments when he enraged me with his exhausting willfulness. I didn't always understand it or even enjoy it. But I was always fascinated by it. I respected it.

I respected *them*. So much press is given these days to today's youth having no respect for their elders, for their peers, for their world. They are accused of being narcissistic, self-absorbed, and reckless. But where are the news stories about how *parents*, so often, have no respect for their children? It is so hard to learn something that has never been modeled.

Once I became a parent, I found that I could not buy into the notion that our children are born to us as amorphous blobs of unrealized potential, and that it is our stringent job to mold them into something useful to society. That they are perpetual works in progress. I agree that we, as parents, bear the holy responsibility to keep them safe and provide them with guidance, opportunities, and a secure base of operations from which to explore their world. But I was never able to accept the idea that we could shape them into our preconceived and idealized versions of toddler, teenager, and finally adult. I *wanted* to, but learned early on, perhaps by virtue of Myles' willfulness as a two-year old, that these boys, at every phase of development were anything but "amorphous blobs" and "unrealized potential." I wrote in my journal when they were just babies—"Please be patient with me. I have never made a man before." I was daunted by the task before me. I never took my responsibilities as a parent lightly—In fact , it often seems, some 22 years down the line, that it is the only important thing I have ever done—but I always felt humbled and awed by the boys. I still do.

I recently stumbled upon a Facebook post that really rubbed me the wrong way and made me feel sad. And though I realize that the piece was intended to be tongue-in-cheek in tone, and darkly comical, I couldn't get past the overall attitude of the post.

The quaintly formatted, beautifully framed post got my attention with the title: *My Promise to My Children*. Aw, I thought. This will be sweet.

My promise to my children – as long as I live – I am your parent first, your friend second. I will stalk you, flip out on you, lecture you, drive you insane, be your worst nightmare and hunt you down like a bloodhound when needed because I LOVE YOU! When you understand that, I will know that you are a responsible adult. You will NEVER find someone who loves, prays, cares and worries about you more than I do! If you don't mutter under your breath "I hate you" at least once in your life - I am not doing my job properly.

This declaration didn't seem funny to me, or clever or the slightest bit prudent. I get that it's supposed to be humorously sardonic. But to me, it seemed hostile and vaguely violent. (I've been stalked before. My own life experience has taught me that when someone "flips out on you," it is never ever a helpful thing.) And though the point is well-taken that we, as parents, don't need to be all chummy with our kids when what they are needing is discipline or boundaries, being a parent instead of a BFF still requires that we show them respect, even when disciplining them. I will never believe that it is necessary to inspire hatred in my children in order to be an effective parent. If they "mutter under their breath" that they hate me, it will not make me proud of myself as a parent; it will break my heart.

Obviously, the parenting techniques espoused here: stalking, flipping out, hunting humans like prey and being their worst nightmare—have never appealed to me in any rendition. These are behaviors for which I would seek serious counseling, if necessary, to avoid. But beyond the ridiculousness of such a parenting approach, I was struck by the self-serving egoism of the vow: *Only when you understand how awesome I, your parent, am, will I respect you as a responsible, valuable person.* Get over yourself, already.

After all that ranting about stalking and nightmares and insanity in this pledge, to state that this is as good as love gets? *No one will love you better?* Damn. That's just depressing, and I beg to differ. There's a whole *world* of love better than that. But will that child recognize it when he/she sees it? If intimidation, bullying, and sarcasm have always been masquerading as love his whole life, what else can he know? What else will she seek?

I *want* my children to seek love. *True*, embracing, generous, expansive love. Corinthians 13 love. And to offer the same. I don't want to limit them with the notion that *my* love, as mighty as it is, is the be-all and end-all for them as they venture out into the world. I hope they *do* find someone who loves and cares for them as much as I do. How lovely would that be?

I think they will. If they haven't already. They are young men now. Out on their own, hundreds of miles away from me for the first time. And still, I feel no need to stalk, hunt or otherwise bully them. Part of that whole "respect" thing, especially as they grow toward independence, is accepting their choices. *They know it when we respect them, they know it when we don't.* Whether or not we put it in so many words, they know. They know by the way we treat them and their friends. They know, more often I think, by the things unsaid than the things we say.

All of this looks really great on paper, as "advice" often does. I admit it was a whole lot trickier in action—on the front. Especially the *adolescent* front—the Waterloo, the Lexington and Concord, the Bull Run—of parenting. But when the stakes were higher, as they inevitably are in the teenage years, it became even more important for me to check my ego at the front line and face whatever skirmishes we became embroiled in with at least the compassion that they offered *me* with their dinosaurs and their Kleenexes.

Ted and I weren't always great at it. We messed up plenty. We too, along with the rest of the world, had to figure out what to do about the whole sex, drugs and rock-n-roll conundrum—or more accurately and frighteningly: the sex, drugs, explicit rap, gun violence, terror attacks, and teen suicides conundrum. We had scary times, angry times, break-your-soul sad times. Times when we felt we didn't even know our kids, and they didn't seem to want to know us. But always, *always*, there was a triceratops or a tissue to clutch in our hands. Always.

The darkest day of my life dawned when my boys were teenagers, 16 and 18. Late on that sweltering Wednesday in July, I dropped my phone without hanging up and forgot how to exhale. I don't remember much else about that moment when my brother told me that my niece was dead.

Jenna, just 27 years old that Monday. Jenna, a true and dazzling star in my cosmos, had drowned in a freak accident in New Orleans, and was no more of this Earth. I scrabbled desperately for my fallen phone and pored over the bantering texts we had shared just days before—as though I could conjure her back to life with evidence of her wit and brilliance and love.

I could not. My phone is not that smart. *I have never known grief so consuming.* Later that night, I wasn't hysterical when we told the boys, but I was crushingly sad. Surely a sad that they have never seen in me. A sad I had never seen in myself. I don't remember going to bed that night.

But I remember waking up the next morning.

I will never forget that morning. Despair seized me the instant consciousness did, and I was overcome by the urge to vomit. But there was nothing left in my stomach to throw up. In the dim light of the hostile morning, I could see pages taped to the back of my door—and on the floor, a small white card. "I hope you are in the mood to read," it said.

I turned the knob on my bedroom door, and suddenly I was Dorothy, opening the front door of my dismal sepia room into the Technicolor of Oz. There before me, everywhere I looked, were notes. Dozens of them. Scrawled in orange, purple, and green sharpie—*notes*, covering, or suspended with yellow yarn from every surface of my house.

Dangling from the ceiling right in front of me, fluttering in the breeze of my movement were six index cards. *You. Are. The. Best. Mom. Ever.* Taped to the wall, in Myles' loopy scrawl, another card—*Buddha would envy your kindness.* On a card on the painting to my right, Taylor's writing—this one had to be Taylor's—*You're cooler than a shark and a bear high-fiving in space!* And next to that, Janna (Myles' girlfriend) had written, *It's hard to be as super awesome as you. Trust me, I've tried.*

Scattered on the floor at my feet were the words, *love, peace, happiness, and harmony*. I stepped over *peace* and *happiness*, and looked up to see drapes of words taped to yarn extending the length of the kitchen from the cabinet above the refrigerator to the faucet at the sink and across the breakfast room to the back door. The toaster said, *smile while you make toast.* On the refrigerator I read, *You're pretty cool! Like a fridge.* The microwave informed me that, *Sadness is part of life. It makes happiness that much more precious.* On the little chandelier over the breakfast table, a secret: *Don't tell anyone, but I think Ted has a crush on you.*

In addition to the words of affirmation and consolation were words I needed even more. Words of everydayness—silliness, family inside jokes and games, music and taunts. How did they know this? How did they *know*, that on this day that was so *unlike* any other day I had ever endured, how did they know, these "self-absorbed teenagers," how did they know that I needed, more than *anything*, the comfort of who we are, who we have been, and who we will be again, as a family, to get me through this time of unimaginable loss?

Somehow they did. On the counter in the kitchen, by a bag of potatoes, they left a card that said, *Lick it,* referring to the lyrics of a Jack Johnson song that Taylor had misconstrued. The lyric, "We can pretend it all the time," in "Banana Pancakes", sounded to him like, "Lick a potato all the time." Another song lyric-- spread out on half a dozen cards or so across the kitchen said, *Beauty. Queen. Of. Only. 18. Sheep.* Another bungled lyric, from a song by Maroon 5. And then on a single card, the lyrics of one of my favorite James Taylor Songs, not bungled (no bungling allowed when it comes to James), *Me and my guitar, always in the same mood ...*

On a line of yarn strung from the breakfast table to the back door, they had suspended nine cards to remind me of the game we constantly played when they were very little. One of us would give the first and last letter of a word in a category, and the others would try to guess the word. Taylor's default answer, no matter what the clues or category, was *dolphin.* I had to smile despite my sad, sad self when I read the cards that asked, *What. Starts. With. Q. And. Ends. In. 5? DOLPHIN.*

They had stuck teasing notes all over our collage of framed

family photos with arrows pointing to each other under labels: *Amazing. Ugly. Decent. The Best.* Or one pointing to Taylor at about 5, picking his nose that said, *He got smarter.* One over Myles as a sturdy toddler that said, *Thug life.* And then, one next to me, sitting under a crumbling archway in Bali: *You inspire happiness, no trait is even comparable.*

All of this and more, oh, so much more. They both had written letters to me and had taped them to my bedroom door. *Letters,* not hastily scrawled notes, but deliberate letters of comfort, validation, encouragement, and wisdom. Yes, wisdom. Wise, wise words from a couple of kids in their teens. Taylor wanted to thank me for making his *time on Earth so amazing.* Myles wrote: *I know you are sad at the loss of your close friend, but I want you to understand that you only lost her in a physical sense. You loved her, and she loved you. There is nothing that exists that can even touch such an unconditional love.* And with these words, I wept with relief of being understood. For Jenna, though my niece by blood, was my *friend* more than anything. My lovely, cherished friend. Myles knew this.

I sat down on the floor surrounded by *love, peace, happiness,* and *harmony,* as the dog padded up to me—*Roof, Bark, Bark, Roof*—she silently said in purple sharpie as she nudged my shoulder. I looked around me through grief-swollen eyes. Those "narcissistic" teenagers had been up all night—not playing violent video games, smoking weed, watching porn, robbing liquor stores, and disrespecting their elders. No. They had been up all night through dawn, taping index cards to strings.

About a year later, on August 17th, 2014, Taylor declined to *live* with me for the first time. He was almost 19. He went away, like his brother, on that grand adventure called college. And again, he was very polite about it, very concerned for my well-being—that innate kindness and compassion still so much a part of who he had become. I tried not to cry too much.

Ah, but that empty nest seemed so vast, so lonely at first. And sometimes it still does. Too much space in this house, too little noise. But I work through it. I have my triceratops and my tissues to keep me company. And that is good enough for now.

It's a Girl
Thang
· · · · · · · ·

Horriblariousness

I crack myself up. I rarely mean to. But I just do the darndest things, and then later—often much later, after I've gotten over the embarrassment—I have to say, I find myself hilarious. Not because I'm innately witty, entertaining, or even particularly clever. I'm funny because I'm a ditz.

I know it's not nice to call people names—even if the people is me, but I just can't find a better way to describe my unique brand of humor. I offer a great deal of comic relief to my friends, family, Walmart shoppers, bank tellers and Chris, my local CVS pharmacist. I can make them laugh. And I don't even have to try. Don't even have to think about it. In fact, the "not thinking" part has proven to be the secret to my comedic success.

It was springtime—and time for our annual "Women's Spiritual Retreat." This was what we called our girl-time getaways. Spiritual Retreat sounded much more respectable than "Get the Hell Out of Dodge" or "Escape From the Husband and Kids." Never mind that the "Spirit" in Spiritual more often came from a bottle than a bible. We needed these escapes. I think most women raising little kids do.

The anticipation and preparation for these events, like Christmas when you're a kid, was often as much fun as the vacation itself. This one was no exception. I was almost giddy with excitement—four luxurious days and nights on the beach in Destin with friends. Cowabunga!

I had bought a brand-new bikini—turquoise with pink flamingos and lace—and I had recently acquired a relatively new body. I had lost nearly 20 pounds the previous year and was back to my happy weight. Feeling good about myself. Maybe a little too good.

The week before the retreat, as I often do before big events, I dieted and exercised fanatically, had my hair cut cute and highlighted, and got a manicure, pedicure and pre-tan.

The day before the big adventure, I had a to-do list as long as my arm. As soon as the kids were on the school bus, I was off and running. Of course, I just had to squeeze in one more workout and a few minutes in the tanning bed, so my first stop was the gym.

During Maria's kick-ass kickboxing class, surrounded by mirrors on all sides, I couldn't help but notice that I was looking pretty good. *Damn good*, I thought. I wasn't quite used to my new, lean body, and my own reflection often took me by surprise.

After class, I ducked into the tanning room, for my final soak in the simulated sun. It was always a bit awkward using the tanning beds at my gym. I found it nearly impossible to be discreet about it, as every piece of cardio equipment in the room faced the door of the tanning room. I would often get dressed and undressed in the dark for fear that someone would barge in on me, and there I'd be, stark naked in front of the entire gym. I was looking good, but not that good!

I emerged sweaty and happy, ready to tackle my to-do list. I pranced out of the gym, past fellow pretty people on life-cycles and treadmills, and out the front doors with a cheery wave to Justin at the front desk.

At CVS I chatted with the cute young pharmacist while I waited for my prescriptions. At the bank, I hollered "Welcome to Bank of America" as I entered, beating the tellers to the punch. (They laugh nervously when I do that.) At Walmart, I sashayed happily about the store, crossing every last item off my grocery list.

I was nearly ready. Just had to head home to pack. I brought all the groceries inside and darted into the bathroom—I had forgotten how badly I had to go, in all my rushing around.

Did I mention earlier that my own reflection often took me by surprise? Well, as I flipped on the bathroom light and started to drop my drawers, I was taken aback. Way aback. Almost tripped over the toilet. I gaped at my image in the big vanity mirror, whimpered a little and instantly learned one of those life lessons you know you'll never forget or forsake.

Never, ever, get dressed in the dark.

My pants were on inside out. My cute little Everlast exercise shorts, once all black, now sported a big white crotch—a glaring diamond shaped thing jutting from between my thighs, up my pubis pointing in the general direction of my belly button. I turned slowly, looking over my shoulder in the mirror at the rear view. Sure enough, the crotch liner inched up my backside where a couple of crisp white labels sprouted from my hiney crack— Everlast®, small, 63% cotton, 27% polyester, hand wash, drip dry.

Oh Lord. How did this happen? More importantly, *when* did this happen? Don't tell me I did an entire kickboxing class like this! No. Everybody in the class would have been blinded by my first round-house kick. And besides, the exercise studio is a virtual funhouse of mirrors. I can't possibly be *that* oblivious.

I finally figured out when the little misadventure began—in the tanning room, not the aerobics room and I was momentarily relieved. *Momentarily.* Then like someone who's lost their wallet, I frantically retraced my perky little steps in my head, feeling sicker with every errand I recalled.

I had pranced all over town, prouder than a frickin' Peacock, with my damn pants on inside out. *Inside out!* Now, I admit I've inadvertently put my thong panties on sideways a time or two, with the cotton crotch up on my right hip somewhere. But no one really had to know about that, as undergarments are typically worn under your clothes. But this, oh this. This was horrible.

It was horrible. For a minute. Then it became hilarious. From horrible to hilarious. Actually, a mix of horrible and hilarious. Horriblarious. What could I do? Boycott CVS, Walmart, Bank of America and the gym? Become a recluse? Move to Jakarta? I couldn't fix it. It was embarrassing, but I hadn't hurt anyone. If anything, I had given some bored box boy a chuckle.

And it really was funny. I recognized that pretty quick. Standing there in the bathroom about to pee in my inverted pants, I could see that I looked absolutely ridiculous. And I knew that I would survive this humiliation. I would live to tell the tale. Others would laugh and take comfort in the realization that their last minor embarrassment—spinach wedged in the teeth, toilet paper stuck to the shoe—was nothing compared to this.

That very few things are too—dare I say, *horriblarious*—to lament for long.

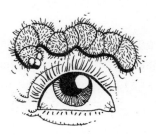

Coiffus Interruptus

I'm cheating. There, I said it. I'm cheating. I'm not proud of it. But it's getting harder and harder to hide. I never meant for it to go this far. I never intended to hurt anyone. I guess that's what they all say—when they get caught. This is my preemptive confession. Thought you'd rather hear it from me.

It all started while you were out of town, of course. Isn't that the way it goes? While the cat's away? I missed you; I always do, but this time was different. Things hadn't been right between us for quite a while. I tried to talk to you about it, but you were always too preoccupied. Couldn't you see that I wasn't happy? My needs weren't being met. The signs were all there. I was just too much of a wuss to lay it all out for you. I knew you'd be hurt. I knew you'd be angry.

It was someone I knew from before. Before you and I ever met. The attraction had always been there. Innocent flirtation. We had never stepped over the line. All these years, and we had never acted on it.

I don't know how it happened. I just couldn't stop myself. I didn't want to stop myself. I fell. I fell hard. I don't know what else to say, except—Goodbye ... Cancel my July 18th appointment for a mani-pedi. I have a new nail tech. And honestly, my nails have never looked better.

I imagined her voice-mail beeping, cutting me off mid-confession. I hung up my metaphorical phone and hung my head—to get a better look at my lovely new nails. Confession is great for the soul, they say.

This wasn't my first foray into the adulterous world of salon sluttery. I have betrayed many a nail tech, hairdresser, eyebrow waxer, facialist, masseuse, you name it. I've jilted 'em. I've left a trail of bewildered beauty professionals all over town. I live in constant fear of running into one of my exes. Because the truth is, I never actually fessed up to any of them. I'm a coward. I just up and left, with no explanation at all. I'm such a cad.

I haven't driven down 12th Avenue since 2003. I can't risk it. Jasmine's salon is in the old Sacred Heart building on 12th. She was my hair dresser for nearly three years, a very long time in the life of a career serial salon slut. I had wanted to leave her for half of that time, but I didn't want to hurt her feelings. And I hadn't yet found a new love.

The truth is, I really liked Jasmine. As a person, I enjoyed her. And that was a good thing. Because Jasmine *took her time*. And my time. And then her next client's time, and then my family's time. The last time she did my hair, I was there for six hours. Six hours. I am not exaggerating. My appointment was scheduled for noon. When I got in my car to go home, the clock on my dash read 5:58.

Now I am not Rapunzel. I don't have tresses to my toes. It shouldn't be that complicated. I maintain a simple, short, bob-ish cut. I require a few highlights, some conditioner, and a blow-dry. What she did up there for six hours is still a mystery to me. But she looked busy. Used lots and lots of stuff—*product*, they call it. And once I was there in the chair, I was kind of committed. Couldn't leave mid-snip. How would that look? Coiffus interruptus. No one wants that.

But it just wasn't working for me. I'd like to say it probably wasn't working for her, either, if only to allay my guilt. But she didn't have a clue. I vanished into the night—okay the Sacred Heart parking lot—with nary a backward glance. I *couldn't* look back; I couldn't move my head. I'd held it in the same tedious position for six hours. Rigor mortis had set in.

It is amazing that I've never run into her. Or Jimmy, my ex-nail tech, for that matter.

His salon was right by Innerlight, the surf and skate shop, and I had a 13-year-old skateboarder for a son. I could no more avoid that shopping center than I could avoid the grocery store. But I was always very stealthy in the parking lot. I didn't actually resort to wearing a disguise—such as my son's Angel of Death Halloween costume—but I did park in the far northwest corner of the lot and then scurried, kind of sideways, like the crustacean Jimmy must have thought I was, into the surf shop. I haven't been caught yet.

And what if I do get caught? What do I imagine will happen? What if I careen right into him there on the sidewalk in front of Innerlight? Will he accost me, burst into tears, beg me to come back and let bygones be bygones? Or will he berate me, make a scene, give me a piece of his mind? Can't you just hear him screaming at me in his inelegant English? *Jimmy best thing ever happen to you. You fool to leave. Jimmy better off without you. You nail look like crap now!*

Or will he just smile politely and say excuse me, because he doesn't know me from a hole in the wall. It's been *years*, for Christ's sake! It is certainly a kind of arrogance on my part to imagine that he remembers me at all. I'm not that memorable, especially since the only parts of me he ever scrutinized were my fingers. I'm not sure he even knows I have a head.

Still, I'm not one to take chances. And I make it a practice to avoid confrontation at all costs. Besides, those nail people can be pretty brusque, and unless you speak fluent Vietnamese, you never know when to take offense or when to take a seat. Or when to take a hike.

I actually had a nail tech seize the Sudoku puzzle I was working on while soaking my nails and fling it across the table. Another tech demanded that my friend surrender his chewing gum—right into her open palm like a stodgy schoolmarm. And who hasn't been slapped silly in the shins when the pedicurist wants you to switch feet. *Now!*

Sometimes, the insults are in English, as was the case when I had my brows waxed by Trina. I didn't notice the huge divot in my left brow until I caught a glimpse of myself in my rearview mirror a few hours later. A little caterpillar undulated over my eye, giving me a palsied yet slightly astonished expression. The next day I went back.

"Look, Trina, it's really crooked, can you fix it?"

She took my chin in her hands, grimly inspected the offending eyebrow and declared, "It not crooked. It you face."

In addition to being insulted, shamed, and bossed around in variety of languages, I have been sweated on by my masseuse, punctured by my nail tech, and bled on by my hairdresser.

Robert was my Seattle hair stylist who nicked himself with the scissors at least once every time he cut my hair, which was doubly annoying, alarming even, considering his HIV status at the time.

In light of all of this, you'd think I'd learn to groom myself. I mean, if my cat can do it, I should be able to make myself presentable without having to employ an army of persnickety beauty professionals. At the very least, you'd think I'd feel little or no remorse when these relationships end.

And end, they do. At this moment, I find myself on the *receiving* end of the jilt. Damn. My beloved Le-Ann, hairdresser extraordinaire, is leaving me. She is ditching me, and there is absolutely nothing I can do about it. I feel so helpless. So alone. So potentially uncoiffed. She is moving to Atlanta. Without me. I learned the news, not from Le-Ann herself, but from my best friend, Vanessa. V was the one who hooked me up with Le-Ann in the first place. I guess she felt a little responsible. I didn't take the news well.

I know I have to move on, get out there, find someone new. But my heart just isn't in it. I've never been good at courting new hairdressers. Once they've cut my hair for the first time, I somehow feel obligated. Kind of like having sex on the first date. *It's not a one-night-stand if you keep doing it.* As soon as they get me in their chair, ask about my kids, tell me about their lousy relationship with their mother, I feel the least I can do is devote myself entirely to them for the rest of my natural life.

Or not. Like I said, despite my honorable intentions, I, more often than not, find myself the rogue. I'm getting quite the reputation around town. Still, I just can't stay away. I need these people in my life. Call me a player. Call me a cad. Call me a sleaze-bag.

And call me if you know the number of a good bikini waxer.

A Bladder Matter

I still can't tell you which is worse. As a flight attendant, I always thought the *passengers* had it made—snug there in their cushy little seats, awaiting their bag of peanuts and cocktail, flipping through the Hemispheres magazine, chatting with their neighbor; while we, their in-flight minions, stowed their stuff, schlepped their trash, and served their snacks. What's so hard about sitting there watching a movie and being served?

It wasn't until I came out from behind the bar cart, and found myself buckling into those "cushy" seats myself as a passenger, that I realized, hey, this sucks. And *I'm* not getting paid to be on this plane, and I'm not getting any exercise, and I need to pee, and I'm trapped.

I had been working as a site coordinator for a company that ran medical conferences for a couple of years, and the air travel was killing me. Even with my Quadruple-Platinum-Trillion-Miler-Hope-Diamond-Studded-Frequent-Flyer status, I wasn't always guaranteed a seat in first class. About a year before I quit this job—largely because of the travel—I chronicled my experience in real time, as I sat there smooshed into that "cushy" seat by the window:

How do I hate thee, airplane-travel-in-coach? Let me count the ways.

Here I sit in 21A, smashed against the window of this ridiculously cramped Boeing 757-200. There are approximately 12 inches between my nose and the seat in front of me. My fancy designer jacket is wadded up behind my lower back. I've just gobbled up three Advil (perhaps the only thing I'll get to eat for the next five hours).

My computer abuts my belly button, so I have to jam my elbows against my ribcage in order to type. I look like a displaced T-Rex, with those itty bitty arms—trying to pet a pterodactyl.

Ms. 20A in front of me just decided to recline her seat. I could easily pick the dandruff off her scalp now. She already stuffed her pink carry-on steamer trunk under *my* seat, as the bulkhead prevented her from having an under-the-seat-in-front-of-you space of her very own. I have room for exactly one peanut on my tray table. My Bloody Mary is taking up the other 3 ½ cubic inches to the left of my laptop. 20A has a vast wasteland of leg-room, and much more tray table real estate than I. I'm feeling a little cranky toward Ms. 20A, but she'll never know because I'm not the type to assert myself and claim my under-the-seat-in-front-of-you homestead exemption.

In fact, I'm not the type to assert myself in any situation that has even the remotest possibility of inconveniencing anyone. I've always been a little proud of that quality. I was the one voted most likely to work and play well with others by a panel of my kindergarten peers. It worked so well back then. Now, not so much. Nobody is rewarding me with an extra graham cracker and Kool-Aid now that I'm a grown-up. In fact, I can't even seem to cajole an extra peanut from the flight attendant. And I'm being so good.

Window seats on airplanes have always distressed me. And not for all those reasons chronicled in the preceding paragraphs. It's actually anatomical.

See, my bladder is miniscule. I know this for a fact. I could actually see it when I went through security this morning at San Francisco airport. Those new-fangled x-ray body scanners are really quite thorough. By the time they were done with me, TSA could rest assured that I wasn't hiding any dynamite behind my spleen. No anthrax embedded in my dental work.

But back to my bladder. It's really one of my most disappointing internal organs (although I'm *quite* impressed with my liver. *Another Bloody Mary, please.*) Any time my bladder and I are trapped against the fuselage of an over-sold aircraft, we panic. We begin to rue the three cups of coffee we had at breakfast (okay, *instead* of breakfast). We beat ourselves up for choosing the slacks without a single pleat. We wish we were a man, a young one with his roomy, accommodating urinary tract. We covet his tidy little prostate—instead of our bulky uteruses that press down continuously, making us squirm with worry and pain. Prostate envy.

In the past, I've tried to *anticipate* this logistical inconvenience, and prepare accordingly. Absolutely no fluids immediately prior to departure. And once on board I wouldn't even permit myself to swallow my own saliva. Around mid-flight I'd feel my skin shrink-wrap my skeleton. My spit-cup would be brimming. These days, I can't be bothered. I need a drink.

Because no matter what I do, *this*: the familiar tingle just below my rigid waistband that turns into a burn that turns into all-out pain and panic. 21B and 21C next to me seem to have recently expired, so dead to the world in their serene slumber, that I probably couldn't rouse them with a Taser (not that I smuggled one on board in my large intestine, thank you very much, TSA).

So, if I ditched my computer, Bloody Mary and peanut, closed my tray table and *squatted* on my seat, could I muster enough force in my quads, enough momentum to *dive* over B and C into the aisle without ending up on D's tray table. Could I? Is it worth a try? I've *got* to do something.

I *so* don't want to awaken these big-bladdered people next to me, but neither do I want to pee in my pleatless pants. I can hold out, certainly, for another—let me check my watch—*another three hours!*

Oh, hell—*Excuse me 21B—EXCUSE ME 21B—**EXCUSE ME 21B!!!***

21B rouses slowly from her coma, registers the panic in my eyes, takes quick note of my squirmy, contorted body language— right leg tucked beneath my buttocks, heel pressed firmly into my urethra—and she gets it. *21B gets it!* Glory Halleluiah, she gets it!

Now, the guy in 21C is the only thing standing between me and sweet release. And he is no match for the two of us. My new best friend in 21B is far less timid than me. Compassionate *and* confident! A true role model. She has Mr. 21C out of his seat almost before he can unfasten his seatbelt. And I'm *off*, waddling urgently toward the light—that lovely illuminated sign in the back of the aircraft depicting boy/girl stick figures with a toilet icon in between. There is no big red X obscuring the toilet symbol.

I am saved.

I can swallow my spit again. I sashay confidently back to my row, where B and C are sweetly, patiently standing in the aisle, allowing me easy access to my cozy little window seat. They're so nice. What could I possibly have been afraid of?

Silly me. I sit down, buckle up, and pick up my Sky Mall Catalog. I wonder if they sell catheters in this thing.

Heavier Things

A ny time lately, when I find myself high on a soapbox, perched to pontificate, I ask myself a couple of really personal questions before I put fresh batteries in my megaphone and start ranting. It takes a lot of self-control to pause and ponder, and I'm rather proud of myself for making the effort. Usually, I get to feeling pretty lonely up there on my wooden crate, and after identifying my true motives, I can step down without having offended, or worse, *bored*, anyone.

Other times (and yes, I'm afraid this is one of them) this emotional autopsy I perform on a touchy issue causes me to learn something really important about myself. Once I've learned something the hard way—through bumbling personal experience—well, then I feel qualified to share my observations.

I don't like the feeling of indignation. It just seems to me that the word itself—*indignation*—is, in real life, almost always paired with the word *righteous*. *Righteous indignation*. Smacks of sanctimoniousness, holier-than-thou-ness, my-god's-better-than-your-god-ness. And for all of that I have little tolerance. I think that I used up all of my self-righteousness somewhere around ninth grade during my stint as a teenage evangelist.

That said, there are situations that get my dander up, so to speak, and I really have to ask myself, "Why?" Why *this* particular thing? Of all the ways I see people disparage and criticize one another in real life, on TV, and on social media, why should I care if someone makes a snide remark under their breath about a total stranger eating a Dove bar walking out of 7-11?

Yes, that is my rant du jour. Actually, my rant du vie. And it's personal.

It takes me back to the kitchen table at 316 Dolphin Street. Takes me back to the hallway at Gulf Breeze High School. Takes me back to myself.

Last year a friend and I were just getting ready to pull out of the convenience store parking lot when my friend, looking up to see a woman exiting the store with an ice-cream bar, smirked, "And I bet she wonders how she got so fat."

Another acquaintance visiting with me on my back deck just a week later, watched as a portly father and son walked down the walkover to the beach with a surfboard. "No way *he's* gonna get up on that thing," she remarked.

My Dad, at 87, still worried that my mom, at 88, *and on hospice care at the end of her life*, was going to get fat. He would hide the cookies under his bed.

Yeah, I have some strong feelings about this. And I am not overweight (usually), unfit or dying. I am like none of these unwitting victims of these snide remarks. And yet, I am like *all* of these victims of snide remarks. And as hard as I try not to be offended, alas, I am.

But why, if I'm not technically in the group being disparaged, why should I care so much? Why do I want to yell at these critics to grow up and be nice? Why do I want to punch them in their little six-pack bellies?

Why? This is where I delve into memories of my childhood.

I feel like I should begin the story of my upbringing with the opening line of Steve Martin's character, Navin R. Johnson, in *The Jerk* ... "I was born a poor black child," because, usually, our recollections of childhood, especially the traumas, are about that accurate.

And by all accounts, even my *own*, my childhood was about as good as it gets in real life—two parents who loved each other, my siblings and me. Nice, clean home. Enough money. Lots of friends. No abuse. A good education. Opportunities galore.

I had many advantages growing up. Still, no one walks away from adolescence unscathed, do they? Some are lucky to walk away from adolescence at all. As I was to learn the hard, hungry way.

If I didn't start eating, they said, I would die. *Yeah, right.* I was 16 and still had another five pounds to lose. What, were they *blind?* Couldn't they see that grotesque roll of fat just below my belly button? Never mind that the scale said 88. I still had a little ways to go.

I would not be fat. I would *not.* I would go so far as to not *be, not be at all*, before I would get fat. I guess I kinda expected them to be proud of me.

Daddy was disgusted by overweight people. Brazenly and righteously disgusted. I'm sure he had other prejudices as well, but this one was pretty much socially acceptable back then in the 50s. At least it was to him. Overweight people were inherently lazy, slovenly and unintelligent. There was no excuse. Over supper, he would often preface a story from work with a description of the obese person he had had to deal with, his revulsion and superiority worn like a medal.

I guess it's not surprising that there was a whole lot of dieting going on at 316 Dolphin Street. My mom and my older sister would sometimes go an entire day or more without eating a morsel. At first I couldn't figure out how in the world they did that. Oh, but I watched and listened and figured it out—and then some. By the time I was 16, I could go an entire *week* eating nothing but lettuce, mustard, and Premium saltine crackers (12 calories each). I win! Yay, me!

Of course, it took a lot more than family dynamics to plunge me into the derangement of anorexia. Overhearing Brenda Harris' mean comment in the hall outside of the biology lab didn't help. It was the beginning of my junior year of high school after summer break, "God, Sharla sure got fat over the summer."

Sharla weighed 114 pounds. I know this because I weighed myself that very day. I was five feet four inches tall—hardly chubby. In fact, today, that weight would put me within about one body mass index point of being categorized as *under*weight. But I grew up in the age of Twiggy (90 pounds at 5'6") and other supermodels like her. So, in the early fall of 1974, I began the diet that could have ended me.

Just a couple of months later, walking through Cordova Mall with my then-boyfriend, Roger, I remember passing by a trendy little clothing store and catching a glimpse of a really, really skinny girl just inside the door. I tugged at Roger's hand and led him back to the shop only to realize that the skinny girl was in the *mirror*, not in the store. Facing my reflection *deliberately*, I could see that it wasn't a skinny girl at all. It was just me. And I could still stand to lose a few.

I feel sad about that. I was never even overweight to begin with, and yet I was able, by sheer force of will, misguided as it was, to starve myself nearly to death. Now it's true that there's a lot of psychological and physiological hocus pocus going on in the mind and body of an anorexic teen that can't be blamed solely on conditioning. But I came by my fear of fat quite honestly.

And it's still quite a sensitive issue.

Just yesterday, at an exercise class at my gym, the instructor casually quipped that if we wanted to feel really good about ourselves and our taut little bodies, all we'd have to do is go to Walmart and have a look around. In other words, go pass judgment on total strangers for a while. Big fun.

That offends me. I stopped taking my Dad to Walmart to get his hair cut for that specific reason. I couldn't stand to listen to it anymore. His revulsion for the overweight bordered on rage at times. And even though he himself, was a good forty pounds overweight, he just couldn't see the hypocrisy.

People love their prejudices. We cling to them like Tarzan on a vine, holding on for dear life and swinging through the world yodeling our defenses of them. Why? I've wondered. But it's really very simple and clear. And sad. We are such an insecure species. We tend to revel in anything that helps us feel superior, smarter, prettier, better, skinnier.

And obesity is just so convenient. So, *in your face*. A person who perceives their weight to be a problem can't keep it a secret; they have to open themselves to ridicule every time they leave the house. So, sadly, many don't. They isolate, often to the point of reclusion.

I have a great many flaws and a great many personal challenges. I have numerous psychological quirks that I am not proud of, some that I won't even write about. But for the most part, I do not have to wear them everywhere I go for everyone to critique.

But what if I did?

I have a friend whose short fuse was threatening to destroy relationships both at home and at work. His temper was out of control. Although never physically abusive, his angry outbursts were alienating those he was close to.

This was an issue for him. And clearly, an issue for the objects of his ire, but as long as he held his temper in check, Walmart shoppers were none the wiser.

I've often wondered though, what if, every time we succumb to our baser instincts and behave in ways not in line with our nobler intentions, what if, every single time we lapse in ways big or small, our physical appearance degenerates? What if my friend grew a small tumor on his face every time he flipped someone off for driving too slow or if his ears grew a little every time he raised his voice with a coworker?

Think about it. Whatever personal challenge you face today, what if every time you mess up, your face gets messed up, or your body contorts strangely. Or you gain five pounds. If we all had to wear our "issues," we'd all look like monsters.

Compulsively over-eating or under-eating are just a couple of ways I have behaved in ways that didn't line up with my values. I can admit that here because I know I am in very good company. We *all* have something. Every last one of us. And, at least for me, it has very little to do with food itself or even the surplus or lack of adipose tissue. It boils down—doesn't it always?—to fear and control.

I know this. I was conditioned early and well, and despite everything I *know* about myself and eating disorders, I still often feel irrationally afraid when it comes to the bathroom scale. It is a life-long battle, even though I am not overweight. But speaking as one who has been perilously *underweight*, it is clear to me that either way, the issue looks like two sides of the same coin. Even with bulimia, in which the sufferer is often neither noticeably over nor underweight, the issue is one of fear, which demands we scrabble mightily for control of something, for domain over something, for superiority over something, anything, anything at all to keep from feeling the fear of being flawed.

A few years ago, a good friend of mine who has always struggled with her weight asked me if, for a hundred thousand dollars, I would gain fifty pounds. I surprised myself with my immediate response. No. No, I wouldn't. How about thirty pounds? Again I said no. I think I gave in at twenty, but my responses made me think.

What am I so afraid of? Everything about me would get to be the same, only I would weigh more—and probably finally own my dream house on the beach. A hundred grand would make a tidy little down payment on a lifetime dream. But no.

And it certainly wasn't because of the possible health implications of putting on a bunch of weight that I declined my friend's hypothetical offer. I didn't even think about that when I blurted out my responses. No, I just couldn't bear the thought of my Daddy or someone like him making fun of me as I cruised the cereal aisle at Walmart, or strolled the beach with my husband, or took a yoga class at my gym. I care too much about what other people think. I am not proud of that quality. But I am proud of my emerging ability to look at myself honestly, even when it's troubling, without having to ridicule or diminish others because of my own insecurity and fear. I don't need to go to Walmart to feel good about myself and my body.

One of my favorite quotes, from Augusten Burroughs, is this: "It is always safe to see yourself truthfully ... People always freak out when they contemplate their own damage or baggage because they think understanding the source, seeing the reason, is dangerous and will make their minds explode or something … But truth is noncombustible."

When people make snide remarks in my presence, what I want to ask them is this: "What are *you* so afraid of?" Every single time I hear these types of comments, *every time*, I look at that person a little differently. A little tumor pops up in my perception of them.

And I know I'm flirting here on the very edge of judgment myself. Guilty of judging the judgmental. After all, everyone is entitled to their opinions. I just wish they could see that I'm onto them. Their insecurity is showing.

Last week I attended a church service in which a ceremony for graduates of a faith-based recovery center was being held. The honorees were men who had completed a rigorous 18-month treatment program for their addictions in lieu of state prison. Their stories were powerful, to say the least. All of these men would be incarcerated, or dead, without the seemingly miraculous intervention of this program, of these devoted people.

Lined up on the stage to congratulate the men as they came up to receive their diplomas were the counselors and administrators of the program, each glowing with pride and respect for these men who had risen to the challenge of rebuilding their broken lives.

Two of the counselors, standing side by side on stage, both beautifully dressed in bright summer dresses, were in all other ways related to stature, opposites. One was tall and very—almost alarmingly—thin. The other stout, and markedly overweight. They were both angels.

They both were in the business of remodeling lives scheduled for demolition. A difficult, often thankless, and truly meaningful vocation. Simply put, they save and transform lives. Not just the lives of the reformed men marching across the stage, but of the families these men are returning to. They are heroic.

But you wouldn't know that at Walmart, would you, Daddy? We *never* know. And even if we did, would we finally see that we are all, in some way, struggling. Maybe it shows, maybe it doesn't. But we all have our crosses to bear.

And I, for one, would rather be the bystander that kneels to help, than the soldier who spits in the face of God's son, or daughter.

·········

Flaw Slaw

Spontaneous Instruction

I'm not sure how it all started, but I know I was addicted by the age of fifteen. Every disturbing detail is meticulously laid out in my writings, and every single journal divulges my compulsion. Every diary, all 208 of them, testifies to my dependence. If I was ever in denial about it, I am not now. The evidence is overwhelming. These journals are my intervention, like dear friends sitting around me in a circle of concern and hope.

Some people argue that addictions are merely habits that have gotten out of hand and can be replaced by healthier, more wholesome behaviors. Others see them as diseases that can only be treated with exactly a dozen steps. I'm not sure which camp I fall into. Not sure what I believe is the cure or the cause, but I know I've got an issue here. A problem that, once and for all, needs to be addressed. I'm fifty-seven years old, for Pete's sake. You'd think I would've gotten a handle on this by now.

I've always been pretty discreet about it. Most people wouldn't even know I have a problem. I'd like to think that my addiction hasn't negatively affected my family and friends. But then, that's what all addicts and 'olics tell themselves, isn't it?

Maybe this is a turning point. A catharsis of sorts. You can't solve a problem until you acknowledge it, can you? *Admitting powerlessness*, they urge. So—in the spirit of twelve steps, let me introduce myself. Hi, my name is Sharla, and I'm a list-aholic.

I've been listing since I was ten, and not a day has gone by that I haven't indulged my habit. I've already succumbed three times today—and it's only 11:00 a.m. The grocery list *had* to be rewritten to better conform to the layout of Publix. My daily to-do list *had* to be updated and tweaked. The stuff I'm taking to Goodwill *had* to be itemized for tax purposes. The IRS requires it. See, I have my reasons. And they are good ones. Maybe a therapist would call this rationalization, but really, it's simply *organization*. Organization is a good thing, right?

I can see in my journals that my listing crossed over from casual use to full-blown list-aholism somewhere around puberty. By 15, I was so far gone that I literally couldn't function without a written mandate. Couldn't even get out of bed without instructions. This is no more graphically illustrated than on the list I made on October 14, 1976 when the first thing on my list was "get up."

Don't laugh. It makes sense. Since every other item on Saturday's list was contingent upon me getting out of bed, it was prudent, if not brilliant, to hold myself accountable. That's what my lists do for me. Hold me to a higher standard of duty. That's a good thing, right?

It's a complex issue. The writing of the list creates a buzz altogether different than *crossing stuff off the list*. Oh, man, I can hardly even type that without jonesing for a pencil. It's like this: If *writing* my list is marijuana, then slashing through those completed items with a really sharp pencil, well that is the crystal meth, the heroin of listing. That's what keeps me going back for more.

I've actually—and I'm a little embarrassed to admit this because it just happened yesterday—I've actually *written in* completed items, tasks that I've already accomplished. All for the rush, that fleeting rush, of crossing them off my list. Pathetic, isn't it?

And isn't this always the case with deviant behaviors: One list leads to another. And not just the next day's to-do list. Oh no, all kinds of crazy lists started to crop up once I had succumbed to the lure of the list. Lists of everything I'd eaten when I'd been on a diet. Lists of everything I'd spent when I'd been on a budget. Lists of everything I'd borrowed and everything I'd loaned. Lists of every boyfriend I'd had (June '75). Lists of every medication I'd taken (November 2008.) Phone lists, book lists, exercise lists, gratitude lists, vocabulary lists. I need an annotated *list* list to keep them all straight.

It's disturbing. On October 13th 1976, I was instructed by my list to "eat" at 2:00 p.m. I had to repeat that behavior on October 15th, but at 11:00 a.m. this time. That was a busy day though. I had to "look for shoes," "take diet pill," "brush teeth," "put bulb in lamp," "shake rug" and "gather poems." Whew! I'm not sure how I managed. I ate 798 calories that day. I didn't spend a dime.

Fast forward oh, say, 40 years. Current list book (yes, I have a whole spiral-bound book for lists): Clean out fridge, write (1 hour), floss, go fishing, and practice piano (30 minutes). As you can see, I *am* a little less rigid though about timeframes. I can pretty much go ahead and floss anytime I think about it. And eating is a little more spontaneous too. I've done that twice today without having to be prompted. I really have no idea how many calories I've eaten. But I know I spent $78.93 when I paid the utilities bill.

It's a good thing that "write" has always been on my list.

Writing has always helped me sort out my problems. Writing this little story has been good for me. I'm not in denial—I know I have a problem. I'm done with rationalizations. I know I need help. But I can lick this thing. If not for me, then for my children. There are so many reasons to quit listing. Among them:

- I will have more time to spend with my family.
- My pencils will stay sharper longer.
- It is the green thing to do.
- I will ward off Alzheimer's by honing my memory.
- I will be way more Zen if I live in the moment.

This is by no means an exhaustive list. I probably have some work to do.

Twig

The twig was broken. There was no denying that. I could see that it was. Snapped right in two, there in Jack's big calloused palm—two almost equal pieces of the tiny stick. Yes, I agreed, it is indeed broken. *Yup, broken twig. I get it. What I'm not getting, however, is why should I care?*

Looking back, of course, I see clearly that not only should I have cared, I should have bolted, run away. Very fast. Without looking back. I should have had a bag packed and ready to go by this time in the relationship. But I was 20-something and "in love" and absurdly adept at ignoring signs—huge signs like those 45 foot tall HOLLYWOOD letters down the road from my apartment that even the most oblivious of drivers on the 101 couldn't miss.

And it's not so much that I didn't *see* the signs. I saw the twig, as small as it was, as huge as it was—but I refused to recognize what that broken little stick implied. A few days earlier it had been the sun visor. Jack had actually walked me out to my Subaru to show me. The sun visor was down. *Yes, I could see that. Uh huh. Right side visor tilted down. And again, why should I care?*

Then there had been the matter of the flashing light on the answering machine. Well, the *had-been*-flashing light. "It's not flashing anymore," he insisted. "See that? It was flashing at lunch.

Now it's not."

Jack was a big man with a small problem, or more accurately, many small problems: twigs, visors, flashing lights. These represented just a few of the bizarre scenarios during the year we were together that should have led me to the same conclusion— Jack had some major trust issues, and it wasn't about me. But at that age (23), in that place (Southern California in the 80s) and with my own slew of insecurities (and delusions), I thought everything was about me. I could fix him.

But that evil ogre, jealousy, ravaged every aspect of our relationship, and instead of stabbing the beast in the eyeball with my broken twig, I—being the ever hospitable Southern girl my mamma raised—well, I patted the cushion next to me. "Have a seat darlin'. Let me get you some sweet tea." I entertained that fiend, that green-eyed metaphorical monster, for years and years—same devil in different guises, on different couches, in different relationships.

And it damn near killed me. At least if Paul had had his way. Paul was another man obsessed with twigs and such, but he did everything with such a charming, disarming British accent, how could I resist falling hard for the guy? I didn't even try. The man was insanely jealous from the start. And I was insanely stupid. I actually moved to London—got a base transfer with Pan Am, packed up everything I owned, and moved in with him.

Only to find myself homeless in the streets of Twickenham less than a year later. I had left Paul with only the uniform on my back and my Pan Am tote bag after I had found that he had been having me followed. When I went back a few days later to collect some of my things, he was waiting for me on the front steps, barring me from going inside. It was clear that I would not be leaving with my stuff, so I turned and hustled back toward the street where my cab was waiting. Paul lunged after me, grabbed me by the arm and spun me around to face him. He was enraged. The cabbie got out of his car and started toward us. Paul shoved me to the sidewalk, stepped over me with a little kick to my ribcage, and stormed back inside the house.

I went to the airport—I had no friends or family there in London. It wasn't allowed. The crew room at Heathrow was the only safe place I could think of. I didn't tell anyone anything. I sat there till dark, then searched the bulletin board in the lounge and found a commuter flat in Hounslow that had an available bed for the night. I was scheduled to work a flight to Los Angeles the next day.

When I showed up for work that morning, my base director, Mark Swenson, took one look at me and ushered me into his office. He asked if I had a long-sleeved uniform blouse in my tote bag. This was odd; it was eighty degrees outside, I was dressed appropriately and according to regulations. He looked kindly at my face, then at my arm. A perfect, black four-fingered handprint marred my right bicep like a tattoo, each bruise deep and distinct.

I had some 'splainin' to do. I did. Then I changed my shirt and went to work.

When I returned from my trip, Mark and his wife took me into their home in Windsor while he finagled a hardship transfer for me out of the country. Despite the emergency protection order in place, Paul stalked me right up until the day before my transfer went through.

I remember my last day in Windsor. I had walked over to Peascod Street by the castle to pick up some things for my flight back to the States. I was heading home to my director's house with my bags, when out of nowhere, Paul appeared like a phantom, haggard and frightful. His eyes were wild and sunken, his beard overgrown. He smelled of Guinness. He grabbed my right arm— still bruised from our altercation a couple of weeks earlier. I screamed, and he hissed at me to shut up. He just wanted to talk.

But there was rage in his eyes, and desperation. As naïve as I was, I knew that my lingering bicep tattoo would have only been the beginning of the marks I would try to hide, and that long sleeves would soon fail to do the trick. His grip tightened. The crowded streets around Windsor Castle didn't seem to subdue him at all. So no, I didn't shut up so we could "just talk." In fact, I screamed again, wrenched my arm free and ran.

He ran after me. He actually chased me through the quaint and cobbled streets around Windsor Castle. I can hardly even picture it now; it's so absurd. But that's the situation I found myself in. Finally, I rounded a corner and barged into the first doorway I saw—a Boots Apotek, a drugstore. The surprised proprietor, seeing my distress, let me duck behind the counter. I crouched there, shaking, for twenty minutes.

The next day, I fled London—yes, *fled*, like an orphaned Syrian refugee—to seek refuge in California. Mark and his wife personally accompanied me on Pan Am flight 102 on a hardship transfer out of the country. I thought I was safe, but within just a few weeks of settling into my new base, while checking my company mailbox in the crew room at the airport, I found a note. Scrawled in Paul's small, meticulous cursive, on a sheet of paper from a Pan Am memo pad were the words, "I know where you live, and we will meet again, and you will be sorry."

Cheerio!

That was more than 30 years ago, and as you might have guessed, I did not die at the hands of an insanely jealous ex-lover. And I wish I could say I learned my lesson that day at Windsor Castle, but it seems I still hadn't had quite enough of being chased around iconic places by madmen. Just a couple of years later, the lovely Pacific Coast Highway (PCH) provided the backdrop for my drama with a man I will call "G."

Who can say why I kept dating the same type of guy over and over and over? I could get all pop psychology-ish about it. I could blame it on my daddy for not being around much when I was a kid or my mom for pretty much checking out of my life when I was a teenager. Or my job, or the era, or my compulsive nature. Or a little bit of all of that. But the bottom line was this: I craved the attention. And when attentiveness turned to possessiveness, then to full-blown obsessiveness, I pretended not to be alarmed. I just knew, clever girl that I was, that these men just loved me *so dang much*. How special I must be to inspire such passion and adoration! And how could I walk out on such devotion? It was like a drug to me. Or a drink.

Or a prescription for antibiotics. It was less than a year later when I staggered, snotty and feverish into Dr. Garza's office there on Torrance Boulevard with strep throat. And I swear I wasn't in flirtation mode. Why, then, did I not think it odd that this young doctor called me at home later that afternoon to check on me— and to invite me to a movie?

From the beginning, Dr. G and I raged around in a perfect storm of relationship drama—me with my daddy issues, he with his mommy issues—against the glitzy, *me-me-me* backdrop of Southern California in the 80s. I put the funk in his dysfunction, and he in mine.

Yes, I was in *LA* now, starring in my very own episode of a cheesy B-movie action flick complete with cops and car chases and blood-curdling screams. *Die Hard* meets *Thunder Road* meets *Psycho*.

The evening started ordinarily enough. We had decided to meet for a drink at Houston's after work. I was on my second chardonnay by the time G got there. As soon as he walked in, I knew he thought he had something on me—the smirk, the swaggery walk, the bloodshot eyes indicating a late night obsessing and drinking. He was still wearing his lab coat. He smelled of Benson and Hedges and stale Aramis. He looked like a young Muammar Gaddafi.

He needed me to confess. *That's all*, he said, *just fess up and we can move forward. He wasn't an unreasonable man; he just wanted the truth.* I remember sitting there, perched prettily on my barstool thinking, *maybe I should just make something up.* But not knowing what it was he thought he had on me, I knew I wouldn't be able to invent an infidelity that matched his imagined one. I was screwed. I didn't know *what* to admit to, but the more I denied his allegations of impropriety, the angrier he got. The bartender shot me a knowing glance and gestured with his eyes to the door.

My thoughts exactly. I pushed away from the bar, snatched my purse from the back of the stool and bolted across the restaurant and out the door, trusting the bartender to take his time with G and the bill.

Once in my car, I pounded my head against the steering wheel a couple of times, then pulled out onto Rosecrans, shaken and nauseated. By the time I got to PCH, I had calmed down a bit. I was sitting there at the red light relearning to exhale when I felt my car jolt, just barely tapped from behind. Things really are closer than they appear in the mirror. It was G. He was literally on my bumper.

And he did not look happy.

The light changed, and I swerved left onto the highway, heading south toward Redondo. And the chase was on. Yes, a car chase. On the mean streets of LA. Well, the slightly perturbed streets of Manhattan Beach. Either way, I was living a Hollywood cliché. I'm not sure what I was thinking—my clunky red Subaru, his sleek black BMW—I had to have known that this could not end well for me. Clearly, I couldn't outrun him; I couldn't go home to my apartment with him chasing me; and I couldn't, or shouldn't, turn right and drive my car across the Strand and into the Pacific Ocean.

I could've used a cell phone, but this was 1985, and besides, I'm not sure who I would have called. By this time, my romance with G had eclipsed most other meaningful or helpful relationships in my life. He liked it that way. And, in some perverse way, I must have, too. I let friends fall away like petals from a cut chrysanthemum. There was no one left to call. No safe place to go.

Unless …

I remembered that the Redondo Beach Police Station was right off of PCH, just a mile or two ahead. I had no intention of trying to have him arrested; he hadn't assaulted me or even verbalized his desire to do so (yet). What would I say to the cops? *Arrest this man! He is being mean to me. And he looks like a Libyan terrorist dictator madman.*

I was pretty sure G wouldn't follow me into the police station parking lot. He, for reasons never fully disclosed, was not particularly fond of "the Man." Despite his carefully contrived doctorly appearance and demeanor, he was a dissident at heart, a frustrated desperado in scrubs trying to make it in LA, after a turbulent childhood in the slums of Honduras. No, he wouldn't invite the police to join our date.

I pulled into the northeast corner of the parking lot, and just as I had hoped, G sped on by. *Hasta luego, machita.* I sat there quaking and pressed both palms into my eye sockets. A sudden tapping on my window jolted me back to reality.

Yes, officer I'm okay. No, officer, I haven't been drinking (much). *I'm sorry, officer, I just had an argument with my boyfriend and I was upset so I thought I'd sit here and calm down before I get on the road. Yes sir, I live in Redondo, just a few minutes from here. Thank you officer. No sir, I'm not in any danger.*

I sat there as long as I dared and then slowly pulled back out onto PCH toward home. I took the long way, scanning side streets and driveways, alleys and parking lots, all the way home. I didn't see his car.

My hands were still shaking when I got to my apartment, and I dropped my keys twice trying to fit the key in the lock of my front door. *Yes sir, officer, I'm just fine. Ha!* I snickered as I pushed the door open, stepped inside my dark apartment—and *screamed* Jamie-Lee-Curtis-style, as I walked full-on into a solid wall of flesh and muscle in the black entryway. A rough hand wrapped around my face and over my mouth. I tried to bite it, but the grip was too strong.

And it smelled like Benson and Hedges and stale Aramis.

He had had a key made. I don't know where or when. It had been on his keyring all along. Somehow that creeped me out as much as the home invasion itself. He had been fidgeting with and fondling those keys for weeks. I had thought it was because it reminded him of that Beemer he could finally afford. But no, I'm pretty sure he was messing with me.

This was a truly, truly terrible relationship. So, of course, a year after this incident, I moved in with him. Yeah, he didn't murder me that night in my apartment so I guess I figured he'd make a good roommate.

That's the bad news, and the relationship ended horribly a few months later. The good news is that this was the last of my truly, truly terrible relationships. I had a few other romances that ended, but never again with cops and car chases and blood-curdling screams.

And *then*, finally, when I was 31, I found a romance that would stand the test of time. And now, a quarter of a century later, it's still standing. We're still standing. (Ted just this minute texted me this quote: "I will love you until I forget who you are." And I think he will.)

I wish I had a formula for finding true love that I could share with you but, truthfully, it could be as simple as this: *I got lucky.* And to hear Ted tell it, surprise, surprise, it would be the same. He'd say, *I got lucky.* And I guess that's the key to our longevity: Reciprocal *I got lucky-ness.* Mutual disbelief over our grand fortune at finding one another.

But with my history of histrionics back then, how in the world was I able to *recognize* and appreciate this good, *stable* man, when I found him among those thousands of fish in the sea? Or hundreds of passengers on the plane. Four hundred and seven, to be exact.

I often joke that our first date was 15 hours long, and we had more than 400 chaperones.

He was seated in the third row of business class upstairs, flight

815. He was wearing a pink shirt, which straight guys did back in 1989. He was reading "Clan of the Cave Bear." He was cute. Very.

Now this is where I could tell you that once I stopped "looking," well, that's when I found my *Mr. Right*. But that would be a bold-faced lie. *I never stopped looking.* I wanted a partner to share my life. I never stopped hoping to find him. And that's why I was so distraught when I *lost* him. So early in our romance, too.

About 20 minutes after I first saw him.

His seat was empty when I came through the cabin to get the bar cart. There were only about twenty empty seats on the plane, and confined as he was to a steel tube hurtling 35,000 feet above the Pacific Ocean, his hiding places were limited. And besides, this 747 was *my* turf. I had worked this flight from LA to Sydney dozens of times. He didn't stand a chance.

Not that he was trying to evade me. He simply didn't know there was a search party out for him. I had enlisted my best friend, Melendy, and another flight attendant to find him. As expected, he hadn't gone far. Just to the main deck cabin to escape the chatty surfer dude seated next to him upstairs. I traded bar carts with Melendy so that I could work his section.

Okay, now I *was* in flirtation mode. I took off the galley shoes I had donned after take-off and put my pumps back on, and I wore them the whole flight.

Falling in love makes time fly—no pun intended. Cloud nine is such a lovely place for romance. Ted and I had 15 hours to charm one another, and we did just that—much to the exasperation of my flying partners. Mellie ran interference for me, but I was pretty useless.

Ted and I connected easily. I was myself, doing what I do. He was himself, doing what he does. There was nothing contrived or premeditated about our interaction (unless you count the high heels), and it felt comfortable but exciting. I loved the book he was reading (*The Clan of the Cave Bear*) and opened with that. He, in turn, was impressed with my new "laptop" that I schlepped with me everywhere. (It was about the size of a microwave and a few ounces heavier.)

Neither of us had had time to prepare for this "date"—this 15-hour rendezvous. But I found such pleasure in his company, and he in mine. I'd say it was delightful. I love what philosopher Alan Watts has to say about it: "To impart delight you have to be more or less delightful. And to be delightful is not some factor of trying to make yourself look delightful. It is to do things that are delightful to you. You become thereby delightful to others. That's to say people who are interest*ing* are people who are interest*ed*."

Ever since my breakup with G, I had been making a point of doing things that were delightful to me. For perhaps the first time in my life, at 31, I wasn't waiting for all of my ducks to line up before I began to live my life in earnest. No, they were quacking all over the yard. And while I wasn't currently in a *romantic* relationship, my entire life was gradually becoming *about* relationships, about connections—with my friends, my work, my writing, my world. I was connecting in a lovely, glistening spider web of associations. I, along with my energetic group of close friends, had begun working with several orphanages in Guatemala City. I was writing for an *Inflight* publication. I was traveling, singing, reading, running—*engaging*. I was *engaging* with the world and the world with me. Ted couldn't resist. He wanted to join in.

Henry Miller once wrote: "Develop an interest in life as you see it; the people, things, literature, music—the world is so rich, simply throbbing with rich treasures, beautiful souls and interesting people. Forget yourself."

And since Ted and I began our relationship in that kaleidoscope of outward connection, it only made sense that we proceed the same way, and continue to this day. We do things together and *apart* that are delightful to us. Yoga and cooking and music and beach-combing *together*. Fishing and volleyball and writing and shopping *apart*.

And in all of our 25 years together, Ted has never once felt the need to wedge twigs under the back tire of my car to see if I'd gone anywhere that day. A tilted passenger-side sun visor suggests that the sun was in my eyes while driving, not a clandestine hitch-hiker hook-up. And the messages (on my answering machine back then, or on my iPhone now) do not concern him one little bit. He's too busy, himself, with that "simply throbbing" world of "rich treasures, beautiful souls, and interesting people."

Of which I am all three to him, and he to me: Rich treasure. Beautiful soul. Interesting person. *Check, check, check*. And it is through our connections out there in the real flesh and blood world that we maintain and strengthen our connection to each other. Wow. I had it completely backwards for so long. To be obsessed over or obsessed with, is not to love or be loved. It is to be sick. And definitely not delightful.

Looking back now, you may wonder if I regret all of those undelightful relationships. After all, one might argue that I had to go there to get here, and I'm really glad I made it here. But the truth is, I *do* regret my part in these romances—my neediness, my carelessness, my feigned obliviousness. I didn't need Dr.

Phil to tell me that "The only thing worse than being in a bad relationship for a year is being in a bad relationship for a year and one day." I *knew*. In each of these relationships, I *knew*. If only on a vague, unconscious level long before the broken twig and castle caper and car chase, I knew that I was living way out of line with my own values. I just didn't have the courage to leave until I found myself toeing a line that, to cross—just one more step—could have landed me in a battered women's shelter. I shudder to think what could have become of me if I'd had no job. If I had had children to consider. If violence had been a part of my upbringing and I knew no better.

So, yes, I regret those times, and I am grateful for that regret, as painful as it was. I seem to be one of those sick puppies that needs to be in a great deal of emotional turmoil (repeatedly) in order to change. And finally, *finally*, instead of saying to myself, "I can change him," I said to myself, "I must change *me*."

And the supreme irony of that was—and is—that in order to change myself, I have to sort of "forget" myself, as Henry Miller urged, and get out of my head and into my world. It is an endlessly recurring theme for me. Occasionally, Ted has to drag me out—playfully pulling me along with him in his adventures. But mostly now I go willingly. Cheerfully.

Delightfully.

My Apologies

I apologize a lot, probably too much. Still, in many instances, it's a good thing. Say, for example, I turn left across Gulf Breeze Parkway, thoughtlessly neglecting to respect your right to continue going straight, and our cars collide. I owe you an apology—and, as it turns out, a bunch of money from my insurance company.

Oh let's say, *hypothetically*, that I reach the end of my rope, and you happen to be attached to it because you are related to me by birth, and I inadvertently instill in you a fear of your own shoes. Well, I should probably say sorry. Really, I should.

And I did. But not until I'd careened off Highway 98 going about 45, into the I-Hop parking lot, slammed on the brakes, exploded out of the car, wrenched open the door to the back seat and quite furiously tied your damn shoes! Okay, so you were only five. Still, I thought you'd understand my dilemma. I was in the *front* seat driving. You were in the *back* seat whining about how your shoes weren't tied right. And the *seam* on your sock—you could *feel* it! I thought it could wait until I wasn't operating heavy machinery. Apparently, you had a sense of urgency regarding the whole situation.

And your shoes got tied. Oh, yes, they did. But my attitude was less than respectful, and for that I apologized.

I have long lived in fear of messing up—and in *terror* of messing up and getting caught trying to cover up messing up. So, these days I'd just as soon tell the truth and apologize up front. Get it over with.

And perhaps save my mom exile to her room.

I was 16. I hadn't been driving long. And I got a ticket. A ticket for speeding. Who'd've thunk my clunky, repossessed Chevy Chevette was capable of exceeding the speed limit? But it did. *I* did. I cruised right through a construction zone on Bayou Boulevard directly into the radar of Escambia County's finest. I was distraught.

And by the time I got to the mall, I was darn near hysterical. Daddy was gonna kill me. My cushy teenage life as I knew it was over. I'd never drive again.

I arrived in a tizzy. I worked at a trendy little boutique between Gayfers and Montgomery Ward, called Bill's Melody. Bill was this *old* guy, probably all of 35, who had his finger on the electrifying pulse of Pensacola's fashion scene—a real celeb. And Melody was his swanky, lanky, glamourous wife. I was awed by both of them.

So, when Bill casually plucked the odious little ticket out of my hands, smiled reassuringly, and said, "I'll take care of it," I was relieved, to say the very least. Just like that—*Poof!* It seemed the whole little misadventure was eradicated. Like it never happened. I would live to drive again.

Fast forward five months. Mom and I were fixing supper. Daddy arrived home from work clutching a Xerox copy of a report. A *police* report it turned out to be. A police report that couldn't possibly exist because Daddy and I had discussed my driving record just a week before when he went to renew my insurance. *No, Daddy, I've never had a ticket.*

Well, apparently Daddy had gone to bat for me. Our insurance agent, a real bigwig about town, former Senator John Broxson, insisted that my record was blemished. Dad gently argued that there must be some mistake. His daughter was not a liar.

Only, his daughter *was* a liar. And John handed Daddy the document to prove it. That evening, Daddy cornered me in the kitchen. The rest is a bit of a blur. Daddy had never been a yeller. That would have been undignified. He didn't need to raise his voice, because lowering it achieved a far more menacing result. He spoke in a deliberate, fearsome growl that expressed his escalating fury quite effectively.

In the 16 years preceding the altercation, and the 40 that have come after, I don't think I have ever had a man that angry with me. And I was afraid. Not of any kind of physical assault—he was not a violent man. But I was shaking. It felt as if my very soul were under fire. And though, to this day, I cannot recall a single word of what seemed like thousands that Daddy said to *me*, I do remember what he said to Mom.

"Frances, you go to your room."

She had come to my defense. By this point, I realized that I did not deserve an advocate, but Mom, being Mom, took it upon herself to step between Daddy and me, "James, let her explain."

"Frances, you go to your room," he growled.

And if I wasn't adequately ashamed *before* her intervention, I was duly mortified as I watched her obey. She turned and slowly crossed the den to her room. I heard her door close.

I don't remember what my official punishment was. By the time that sentence was handed down, I was already serving hard time for felony disgrace. It was clear from the onset of this altercation that I had embarrassed my father badly. When he turned around and passed that humiliation onto my Mom, I was doubly culpable.

I carry that shame with me today. I regretted disappointing my dad, though my teenage brain didn't want to admit it, but it nearly *killed* me to cause my mom such indignity. She had been banished, like a disobedient toddler, to her room.

"Frances, you go to your room."

And she went. Without another word, she went.

I'll never know how she felt about that; we never discussed it. But that exchange, for better or for worse, or maybe for better *and* for worse, has shaped my behavior ever since. I'm pretty good at accepting responsibility for my screw-ups, even *before* I get caught by a cop, a senator, or my Dad.

I apologize. I am so ready to admit fault that I have found myself formulating my apology in my head even before I have messed up. Just in case. Certainly that kind of thought process undermines my confidence, but I can't help it. I don't want anyone to be sent to their room because of me.

But the upside is this: I tell the truth. When my insurance company asked me why I turned left onto Gulf Breeze Parkway and crashed into an oncoming car, I told them it was because I wasn't paying attention, certainly not the explanation they were fishing for. When they prompted me to state that the other driver could have done something to avoid hitting me, I told them that I really hadn't given him a choice.

And of course, I told them how sorry I was about the whole thing.

Shallows

Oh, me of little faith. I want to believe that I can do this, that I am not alone. I want to believe that I am protected and empowered by the divine. But sometimes it's just so scary, and it's hard to make myself step back into the current, the flow, the tide that never stops moving. After a deep disappointment, a departure, a death—after grief has had its way with me—I find myself transfixed on the shore.

Life goes on. I must rejoin. I know this, but I'm afraid.

It looks so rough out there today. A southwest wind will do that if it blows long and hard enough. It seems to make the Gulf angry. The waves are enraged. The currents are riled. And I'm afraid of all that turbulence, but it's not because I fear it will sweep me away. No, the waves are pressing mightily *toward* shore. I guess I'm afraid of being dashed back into the sand where I started—to be tangled in seaweed and mangled in broken shells. No, I don't fear some dark danger in the unknown depths out there. I'm afraid of the quotidian, the *same*, the banal and trite. I'm afraid of the shallows. I'm more apt to perish there than in the deep.

Things *break* in the shallows. Just look at those waves close to shore. They have to spend their energy by crashing. There is nowhere else to go; nothing left to do but break apart on the beach.

Look at the paradox. Look at the way the depths seem calmer, richer, more solid. The shallows, all agitated, disordered, rough. Out beyond the surging waves, the flying foam, things calm down a bit. I can see it. But it's just so hard to get there from here. It takes courage I never feel I have.

I *do* know how to swim. I *am* strong enough despite my sorrow. But when I get in turbulent water, I often panic and become frantic for the shore. I'm tired of flailing, of turning back, of struggling futilely against these churning tides. I want to arrive at some place *better*. Not right back where I started, exhausted and bitter. Let my grief at least do that for me. Deliver me to a deeper place.

And looking out over that raging seascape from the deck this morning, this emerging metaphor exasperates me: *There is no way for me to get to a depth that is comfortable to me—but through the shallows.* I guess I already knew this. I've had to learn it the very hard way. Still it pisses me off. So, what now?

Maybe I will struggle some more. Or maybe I will be brave and calm enough to dive deep—underneath a lot of the messiness. Either way, I will come out of my room, out of my head, and step back into this life this morning. This mourning.

This shallow, deep morning, and flow. Or flail. Or maybe walk on the waves like Jesus on a Galilean Sea.

Messy
Mortals

. . . .

Moonshadow

I t wasn't actually *instant* karma, I suppose. The woman had been around a long, long time, and this clearly wasn't her first rudeness rodeo. She'd apparently had a lot of practice. So what happened to her may have been a long time coming. But to me, having enjoyed the displeasure of her company only for the short duration of our plane ride from LA, it seemed like swift justice, prompt retribution from the Universe. Don't you just love it when that happens?

I have to admit, *I* do. I feel a little guilty about that. After all, what kind of lousy person rejoices in the misery or humiliation of another, especially a frail elderly woman alone on an airplane?

This kind, it seems. Because this story is just too funny not to tell. Still, I'm a little uncomfortable with it all. I'm not the kind of person who finds it hilariously funny when someone slips on a banana peel. I have a close friend, probably one of the most compassionate human beings I have ever known, who absolutely cannot restrain herself, even though she tries. When someone trips and falls, steps in a puddle, or otherwise fumbles or stumbles, she cannot suppress a giggle. Or guffaw. She just can't. Though she is never cruel, always kind, and the very first on the scene to pick you up and dust you off, the slapstick nature of a good tumble really cracks her up. For this reason, I never wear high heels when we go out together.

See, I'm a bit of a bumbler myself. Maybe that's why *America's Funniest Home Videos* distresses me so. Even though I don't have a pair of my own, I put a pillow in my lap every time they show one of those video montages of guys getting gonged in the gonads.

I'm always of the there-but-by-the-grace-of-God-stumble-I mindset. It could be me. Never mind that I'm anatomically protected from testicular trauma. There are plenty of other ways for me to embarrass myself, and I do so regularly.

So, it is with mixed emotions that I tell you about the old lady in 1A. I'm surely making her out to be much meaner than she actually was, in order to justify my delight in her demise. But she *was* a cranky little thing.

She hobbled onboard imperiously—if such a thing is possible. Though frail-of-frame, she was clearly arrogant-of-attitude, barking orders at the flight attendant to stow her Tumi tote and get her a drink.

She was dressed to the nines, maybe even the elevens or twelves: royal blue Chanel-ish suit, crisp white ruffled blouse, glistening gold bangles, baubles and belts—and I swear, what looked like Jimmy Choo orthopedic pumps. Even her cane was polished and gleaming, and it thudded to a halt right there at my feet. Of course. 204 open seats on this spacious 767, and Ms. Sweetness-and-Light is *my* seatmate.

Oh yay.

Disgruntled. That's the word Pan Am training material used back in my flight attendant days to describe the "problem passenger." She was the poster child for *disgruntled.* I don't know what they subjected her to out there in the boarding lounge—Chinese water torture, colicky quadruplets, Sonic Drive-In commercials? I don't know, but it must have been really awful.

Or maybe they just didn't let her pre-board with the rest of first class. Yes, that was it, as she loudly confirmed, harrumphing her way into the seat next to mine. They made her board in zone *one*, the morons.

And if that wasn't bad enough, they had seated her (here in the first row of first class) at a *bulkhead*, depriving her of the under-the-seat-in-front-of-you stowage space which is her frequent-flier birthright. That rant lasted about a minute. Thirty seconds longer than her Dewars and water.

Up to this point, I had yet to utter a word. *Maybe she'll think I'm mute or deaf or otherwise impaired and leave me alone.* I briefly considered drooling a little, to further discourage any interaction, but opted instead for the I'm-so-engrossed-in-my-Sky-Mall-catalogue-I-can't-tear-my-eyes-away-to-acknowlege-your-existence ruse.

I felt a little bad about this, too, as she clearly was needing a full-time, interactive scapegoat. So, she immediately began to harass the poor flight attendant again. She needed another drink (*Today, if you please*), her carry-on from the overhead bin (*Within the calendar year, if you can manage it*), a blanket (*in the sealed, unpunctured, plastic wrapper*), and a fresh *Delta Sky Magazine* (*Some illiterate idiot has already half-filled in the crossword puzzle in hers*).

Oh Lord. *How much longer till we land?* Hard to say, as we had yet to take off. It was going to be a long night. I didn't know how much longer I could feign fascination with Talking Smurf Toothbrushes, Bigfoot Garden Yeti Statues, and Cat Topiaries.

Finally, the boarding doors were closed, the Captain announced we'd be on our way, and the flight attendant began preparing the cabin for take-off, which, unfortunately, included wresting my seatmate's cocktail from her arthritic claws. This set off yet another tirade that the flight attendant didn't even hang around to listen to.

I couldn't blame her, of course. I had been in her position more times than I could count. It had been nearly two decades since I had had to sweetly endure the remonstrations of the chronically disgruntled passenger, but it all came flooding back to me as though it were yesterday. What is it that makes people behave so boorishly on airplanes?

Once, aboard a Pan Am flight to London, I had a passenger in First Class threaten to "write me up" for not doing anything about the turbulence that made it impossible for her to paint her toenails. On a flight from New Zealand, I found myself as the chief purser in a sudden death scrimmage with an entire professional rugby team, who thought it would be hilarious to commandeer the PA system from various jumpseats while we were serving lunch, and make lewd announcements to a planeload of 400 family vacationers. I have to admit, for big guys, they were pretty stealthy. (They were no match however, for the armed security agents I requested once we landed in Sydney.)

Yes, the travelling public could be unreasonable, cranky, and crude. And impossibly presumptuous, especially when cultural lines get crossed. On a flight from Bombay, a sari-swathed, jewel-bedazzled Indian woman in Business Class held her fragrant baby up to the flight attendant commanding, "Change her." When he returned minutes later with a different baby in arms, she was not amused when he asked, "Will this one do?"

But I digress. Back onboard Delta Flight 1537 with my new friend, it was dinnertime. Having served literally thousands of in-flight meals in my day, I thought I had been privy to every conceivable way to disparage airplane food. Shows how much I know. You'd think the flight attendant had set a heaping plate of mad cow offal in front of her.

Clearly, when dealing with the flying public, a strong talent for compartmentalizing unpleasantries, a solid poker face, and most importantly, a sturdy sense of humor are all valuable assets.

It was tough though to find any humor at all with Her-Haughtiness grousing and grumbling with every exhalation of her boozy breath. At *first* anyway. But like the prelude to a really good punch line portends—*wait for it, wait for it*—both the flight attendant and I were eventually richly rewarded for our patience and restraint in dealing with this, the Queen of the Disgruntled.

We just had to wait until she fell asleep.

And finally she did. *One* filet mignon, *two* hours, and *three* scotches later, her beady little eyes drooped shut, and she was out. It's hard work being that ornery.

I must have dozed off as well. It was dark and quiet in the cabin when I felt a gentle nudge on my shoulder and looked up to see the flight attendant, eyes wide, gesturing discretely to my slumbering friend in 1A.

Oh, Lord.

Her teeth had fallen out—and were dangling from her bottom lip. The one tiny dab of Poligrip that had refused to abandon ship was hanging on for dear life, valiantly keeping those choppers from falling into her cleavage.

And suddenly, from out of nowhere, that old Cat Stevens song, "Moonshadow," started blaring in my head—something about losing my mouth, and my teeth, north and south—and I felt a totally unwarranted, undeserved surge of compassion for this woman I had come to loathe, and I wanted to take my index finger and discretely poke those pearly whites back up into her haughty head where they belonged.

But I didn't, of course. And neither did the flight attendant. In fact, we both did exactly what you might expect us to do. Nothing. Nada. Zip. Zero, Zilch. This was either a very passive response or a very noble one, depending on your perspective. We didn't help, but we didn't hinder. We did not take a picture and post it on Facebook.

The flight attendant grinned, shrugged and went back to the galley. I gawked a few seconds more, then closed my eyes and let Cat Stevens serenade me back to sleep. When I awoke, all was well with the world. Molars, canines, and incisors had all been reunited in her mouth, and for the first time all flight, it was closed. We did not hear a peep from her for the rest of the flight.

And the moral of this story is what? Be nice? Don't forget to floss and have regular dental check-ups? Learn to sleep with your mouth closed? I dunno.

But if I ever lose *my* mouth, or any associated dental work, and have to get *me* some dentures, I'm using Gorilla Glue to secure those suckers.

ESM

O kay, so what's the worst thing anyone ever said to you at a party? I can top it. A few years ago, at a baby shower, I was asked if I was my best friend's mother. Vanessa was 41, I was 47.

Now, there was more than one way I could have looked at this. I could have gone with my initial response—*do I really look that bad?* Or opt for the kinder, slightly less painful reaction—*does Vanessa really look that good?*

Okay, V did possess a youthful, natural physical beauty to match her personality; there's no denying that. But realistically, she would have had to be about 25 for me to have given birth to her. On the other hand, given her true age of 41, if she *were* my darling daughter, I'd have had to be about 65.

(Now, I knew that I was looking a bit haggard when I woke up that morning. I was on the tail end of a nasty cold. I finally felt well enough to leave the house, and it actually felt good to get out of my sweats and into my party dress. I got all dolled up for the event. Even wore eye-liner.)

But anyway, back to the math. If we split the difference— say maybe Vanessa looked about *35*, which was more than reasonable—I still would have had to be somewhere in my mid-fifties. And as is always the case, any decade beyond the decade I inhabit, seems geriatric. (Fortunately, the line keeps moving, and my fifties aren't the doddering decade I feared at the time. But man, I'll be *old* in my sixties.)

Still, I wasn't feeling much better about the whole thing sitting there sullenly on the sofa nibbling pink petit-fours, sipping pink punch. Vanessa, bless her heart, her nubile heart, was mortified—flattered, perhaps, but mortified nonetheless, for my sake. Come to think of it, maybe she wasn't even flattered, given the *source* of the compliment/assault. When I told her about the insult (through tears or laugher, I can't remember) she immediately knew who the offender was.

The Evil Stepmother.

I kid you not. It was the evil stepmother, the notorious nemesis of Jenny, the young (yes, actually *young*) mother-to-be whom we were all celebrating. The stepmom's notoriety, it seemed, stemmed from her utter lack of tact. *Ya think?*

I don't want to be catty. Or actually, maybe I *do* a little, but she was quite the frightful sight. Seems she had recently undergone gastric bypass surgery and apparently had lost a few hundred or so pounds but had been largely unsuccessful at giving all those extra chins the slip. (That was mean, I know—I can't help it.) She was louder than the average baby shower attendee, and seemingly not well-versed in the fine art of making light conversation with total strangers. In our first (and next-to-last) conversation she let me know how relieved she was that her developmentally disabled daughter-in-law—who was seated next to me—and her developmentally and physically disabled son, had chosen the vasectomy route. *Had them nads neutralized, praise God!* Snip snip. We went on to discuss her son's testicles for a few more minutes before we moved on to the subject of my genealogy. That's what

I get for being a lousy listener.

So, you must be Vanessa's mother ...

When others at the party heard of my disgrace they were tripping all over themselves to comfort me with tales of the *ESM's* gaucheness, tackiness and general white trashiness. I appreciated their concern for me. I'm a little ashamed to admit that their comments were comforting.

Still, for all the welcome slanderous remarks made of the poor woman, only *one* would have made it alright for me—that the woman is legally blind.

Flower Power and the Mean Girls

I did something in the bathroom that I'm really ashamed of. And it wasn't even my bathroom.

This stuff is very hard to write about. But it's time to come clean, even though *I* wasn't the one in the shower. I *was* there in the bathroom; I'll admit to that. Still, if I had known then, at 12-and-a-half, what I know now, I wouldn't have gone over to Lorna's at all. I should have known something was up when I saw Cameron and Claudia making out in the middle of the road in front of her house. But I was too excited. I was hanging out at *Lorna's*. And she was the most popular mean girl in school.

I'd had a crush on Cameron for almost a whole week, and Lorna knew it. Katherine had told her. Katherine was *my* best friend. Claudia was Lorna's best friend. Lorna put Claudia up to it, just to see the look on my face when I saw them there in the middle of Shoreline, sweaty limbs all tangled up, devouring each other's faces. I had never seen anyone making out before in real life. Just on TV, like Andy smooching with Helen Krump in the back of Barney's squad car. But this looked way more slobbery than that. I pretended not to care.

Lorna had witchy straight black hair that she usually wore in a stark part down the middle of her scalp. She was pale and freckled and mean as a snake. She was darkly popular, a middle-school dynamic that I have yet to understand. She was scary. And everybody wanted to be her friend.

I was shocked when she invited me to her house. She had shown up for school one day with those thick back locks pulled back in a tight French braid. I had complimented her. A couple of days later she offered to teach me.

My friend Katherine had been hanging out with her some lately; they lived on the same street. That connection emboldened me a little, though I was still pretty nervous as I tapped on the door, using the hair elastic I had brought—the kind with the little acrylic balls attached—as a knocker. Lorna ushered me in and hollered to Claudia, still there in the road with Cameron, to come on.

I walked into the dim foyer and was led directly to the hallway bathroom. It was brighter in there, decorated with yellow and orange towels and a flower-power shower curtain. Smelled like Jean Nate and urine.

They sat me down on a stool in front of the sink, and I watched in the mirror, hardly believing my good fortune, as Lorna pulled a sturdy brush through my slick blonde hair. *Unreal.* I thought. I'm at Lorna Parker's house, and she is *brushing my hair! This is unreal.* If only I'd known then how truly unreal this whole adventure was, how totally false it was from the start, I'd have taken my balls—on my new elastic hair tie—and gone home.

I would like to think I was clueless back then. I was so small and innocent. But looking back, I can see that I was "clue avoidant," if anything. Didn't want to see the writing on the wall—or on the shower curtain, as it were.

Claudia sat on the edge of the tub behind me as Lorna began weaving my hair.

"Can you believe what Amanda was wearing today? She is just so groady. And she smells like feet."

Lorna laughed and gave a little tug on my hair so I'd laugh too.

Amanda was the poorest girl in school, and though we had been in the same fifth grade room the year before, I had never heard her utter a word. Not a syllable. Even Mrs. Williamson ignored her, never once calling on her in class. Amanda sat across from me all year—our desks were arranged in a big horseshoe— and she was directly opposite me. Still, I do not remember anything about her face, except the early acne. Her hair fell in greasy, tangled clumps over her desk, and she rarely looked up. She did smell bad, and I felt sad for her.

(I thought of her as the years passed. At my fifteen-year high-school reunion, I remember fantasizing that Amanda might show up, dazzlingly beautiful—slim and tan, with a handsome husband and a career in broadcast journalism. She would have two perfect children and a silver BMW. Lorna would be in a crack house in Compton.)

"And *Katherine*," Claudia went on, "What's with those stupid pigtails she wears every day? What is she, *seven?*"

Lorna caught my eye in the mirror and waited, eyes narrowed, for my response. I had been nearly mute since I walked in. Now I was expected to weigh in. Katherine was my best friend. Surely I'd have something to say about those stupid pigtails.

But I loved those stupid pigtails. In fact, I loved everything about Katherine. She was the most interesting person I had ever met. She was the second-oldest of nine kids in her family. She taught me to recite all of their names in order. Their house was huge and rambling and cluttered and noisy and kind of smelly. I used to take an empty Dove soap box with me on sleepovers to press to my face at night when the smell of wet diapers was too much.

They went through lots and lots of diapers, and Katherine, as the oldest girl, could change a diaper without even looking up from her book. She always had a book. Always. And her imagination was always revved and ready to race. We were still young enough to love H.R. Pufnstuf (though I never would have admitted this to Lorna and Claudia) but teen-agey enough to be "in love with" the Beatles; Katherine with Paul specifically, me with George. We had crazy adventures in the sand dunes next to my Aunt Lorraine's house, making up elaborate scenarios involving not only Paul, George, and H.R. Pufnstuf, but also Jack Wild, Davy Jones and sometimes, Marcia, from the Brady Bunch.

So what about those stupid pigtails?

I don't remember the specifics of what came next. I've blocked it out from shame, so it had to have been pretty bad. I think we badmouthed Katherine for at least ten minutes, with each affront crueler than the last.

Finally, the girls exchanged mean and meaningful glances in the mirror, Lorna nodded, and Claudia, with a dramatic flourish of her scrawny arm, whisked back the pretty shower curtain behind her, and there stood Katherine in the tub, fully clothed, stupid pigtails and all, motionless and bewildered.

And this is where this memory crashed. It was so long ago, but it baffles me that I can remember the daisies on the shower curtain, the ammonia and lemon stench of the cramped bathroom, the metallic scrape and jangle of the curtain rings on the rod, but not the look on my best friend's face. I don't remember what I did next, or what Katherine did next or what the mean girls did next. I don't remember leaving.

It is an awful memory that has served me well. I got to learn, at twelve, what it feels like to be a real shit. There was no way around it. I was a mean girl. If only for those few moments, I was one of them. And I hated myself for it.

I'm still working on redemption, 45 years later. And the imagery of that shower curtain being swept away to reveal my friend has stayed with me, and I conjure it up intentionally anytime I find myself pulled into a conversation that I have no business having. There is a real person behind the curtain, one who deserves my respect and loyalty.

No one thinks of themselves as mean. And when pressed to admit to *doing* something mean, everyone I have asked has drawn a blank. It's just too ugly to look at. Now, most *everyone* I talked to could come up with a story about meanness, but in most of their accounts, they were the victim, not the perp.

I've got a few of my own victim stories. They are easier to tell than the ones that feature me as a jerk. Of course they are. There is very little shame and quite a lot of righteous indignation involved in recounting the way someone has hurt *me*. How dare they?!

How dare *she?* Just a couple of years ago, I was the baffled victim of some very bad behavior. Do we really need any more poor-me, victim stories? Well, maybe—maybe not. But this one matters to me, because, like the girl behind the shower curtain incident, it really changed me. For the better. Yes, I am a better person for having been both deceived and deceiver, insulted and insulter, used and user.

"Anita" and I met through work—thrown together on a project that we were both passionate about. She was very creative, talented, and energetic. I was a little needy and forlorn, making my way clumsily through those seven stages of grief—lingering on number four, as the depression and loneliness of losing my dearest friend two days before Christmas pummeled me like a fist every time I uncurled from the fetal position.

In many ways, I was as vulnerable as that twelve-year-old in the bathroom and even more oblivious. And again, just like in middle school, there in middle *age*, there were clues. There are always clues. And still, *still*, I was pitifully "clue avoidant."

My neediness overwhelmed my common sense and I ignored signs that even my preadolescent self would have found troubling: cruel texts she showed me she had sent to an estranged friend, snarky remarks about a trio of overweight women on the beach, the occasional racist-ish idiom popping up in conversation. I tried to dismiss it all with the "nobody's perfect" defense, but I was becoming increasingly uncomfortable. Still, every time I tried to back away a little from the relationship, I found myself tripping over her good qualities, of which she had an abundance.

Ah, yes, another lesson. There are no all-good people. There are no all-bad people. But the balance got tipped abruptly to the latter with another careless text. Would she ever learn? No, no, she wouldn't, as you'll see. This text made it to my phone, rather than its intended recipient, quite by accident. That send button is obedient only to touch, not intention.

This errant text, while clearly not intended for me, was sickeningly revealing. The two-paragraph text divulged to me some new insights into Anita's character that were very disturbing. The missent text also revealed that she had planned to involve me, without my knowledge, in some shenanigans I wanted no part of.

Now, I must confess here that there is a part of me that wants to transcribe that naughty little text word for word for your reading enjoyment. You'd love it. It was a doozy. And, as luck would have it, I just *happen* to still have it, saved on my phone. (Interesting thing about smartphones; they can hold grudges for you absolutely as long as you want.) But to do that, and risk hurting others that were unknowingly involved in her drama, would drop me squarely back into the mean girl camp, and hey, I'm the *victim* here, stupid pigtails and all.

Anita, when she realized her mistake, was mortified, embarrassed and apologetic. I let her have her say, I had mine, and then I tried to bow out of the friendship subtly, over time. When that didn't work, I just told her, face to face, as kindly as I could, that the relationship was just too complicated for me at that time in my life. And this was true: I was still grieving the death of my niece and my dear friend, my mother was dying, and my brother had just been diagnosed with a serious heart defect. Even *she* could see that I had a lot on my plate, and just didn't have it in me to belly up to her buffet, too. Still, I sincerely hoped that she could straighten everything out. But I didn't plan to be around to watch.

Turns out, what *I* thought was a period (actually an exclamation point), punctuating our friendship, was only a comma to her. About a month later, six days before Christmas, on my birthday, I arrived home from work to find an extravagantly wrapped stack of presents on my doorstep. How could something that usually fills me with the glee of a kindergartner suddenly overwhelm me with sickening dread—not that I anticipated anything but thoughtful loveliness inside those pretty boxes. She had great taste and was very generous. The gifts would be great.

But I wasn't drinking that Kool-Aid anymore. I had sworn off the stuff. To even *acknowledge* the gifts would be taking a swig. To send them back to her would be *dousing* myself in it. To ignore them would be boorish. Which is exactly what she was counting on. Exactly. And I knew it. But I didn't know what else to do, or not do, as it turned out.

And it turned out that she had orchestrated a golden opportunity here, to turn the tables in this stupid game and make *herself* the victim. The victim of my thoughtlessness. What kind of rube lacks the decency to say thank you for gifts received?

This kind of rube, I thought. Oh, yes, *this* kind, for sure. And this was tough for me. I have elevated the practice of writing thank-you notes to an art. I have even written a thank-you note in response to a particularly lovely thank-you note. So, it killed me to leave the gifts in their boxes and say nothing.

Killed her too. Not long after New Year's, I got the text—yes, again with the texts. *What about the presents?* And as reluctant as I am to engage in arguments using only my thumbs and technology, I responded in kind, with a text of my own. Face to face conversation had failed to get my point across. Maybe this, her preferred method of communication, would. Still, not wanting to risk hurting others, I tried to be discreet in referencing her little drama, I wrote:

> *Anita, I'm frustrated that I'm in this position of being the ungrateful bad guy. Yes, the gifts were lovely but, Anita, I don't want this relationship. I don't know how else to say it. I hate being in this position, having to say this again. Please respect my wishes. If I'm the only casualty of your situation, count your blessings. Please. I will always be friendly when I see you. I want good things for you,*

but this relationship feels unhealthy to me. Maybe I'm wrong, but I have to go with my gut.

These were my exact words, according to my handy little grudge-keeper. Her response was immediate and ruthless. These are *her* exact words—as typed on her handy little relationship crusher:

Hey. All I wanted was a thank you. I do not want a relationship with you, Sharla. I have NO use for people that are hard hearted and unforgiving as you are. People fuck up occasionally. I am a wonderful Loving Forgiving Soul who will always give people the benefit of the doubt. Don't flatter yourself thinking that I want to be your friend. I don't. I've just NEVER known anyone that hasn't responded with at least a thank you for something I've given them. That's ALL I expected. Not a dissertation …

And then, my very favorite part:

You are not as nice as you think you are FYI.

Ha. Oh my. Oh my! She certainly told me! I was speechless—but not quite textless:

Wow.

Lovely.

That was not a great idea, Anita.

Bye.

And my husband—my big, strong, sweet, protective EagleScoutMan promptly blocked her from my cyber life. And changed the combination on the door locks. And got me a new car. And set me up in a witness protection program. (Okay, that last one, not really. But he did get me a new car.)

It was really creepy. To be hated like that—with such precision and intended malice. Especially in light of the fact that I had some really, really, smelly dirt on her as revealed in her errant text that—come to think of it—I could pull up on my phone at any time. Why would anyone want to incur the wrath of the one person who could let a whole legion of feral cats out of their bags? Perhaps she knew deep down, even then, as she accused me of hard-heartedness, that I wouldn't do that. (Even though I know you're dying to know the sordid details, I still won't.)

But I was rattled that day. Truly unnerved. I would like to say that I was able to *shakeshakeshake* it off in a perky little dance number, but it was very, very disturbing.

And hilarious. Disturbing and hilarious. (Let me try this again: *Disturbilarious!*) Very few insults can withstand a blitzkrieg of humor. I didn't know it yet, but my troops were standing by, ready to storm the beach with me.

I had become fixated on her parting words to me, the sharp, poison-tipped little PS in her text: *You are not as nice as you think you are FYI.* I knew that *she* knew, that of all the slurs she could hurl at me, this one had the potential to hurt me the most. Yes, even more than "hard-hearted and unforgiving." She knew me well enough to know what some of my deepest-held values are, and that I had been trying (like the Dalai Lama, but without quite as much success, apparently) to embrace *kindness* as my religion. Thank you, Lorna. Thank you, Claudia. I've been seeking redemption for 45 years. Kindness is my penance.

I recall some suggestions outlined in Deepak Chopra's *The Book of Secrets*, describing specific, active ways to actually *practice* kindness and other spiritual aspirations. Under the *Giving* caption, he recommended that I "compliment someone for a quality that I know the individual values in him-or-herself." That's if I want to *give* to others. If I want to assault and devalue others, if I want to *take away*, then the opposite approach works nicely. Just ask Anita. She was perceptive enough to know what mattered to me and mean enough to know precisely how to go for the jugular.

I'm not as nice as I think I am? Well, this *is* perplexing, truly. Since I'd never spent a whole lot of time *quantifying* my niceness or lack thereof, I didn't know my baseline. I needed to know how nice I think I am in order to know how nice I'm not. Sheesh. It's complicated being me.

Yes, processing this whole thing was a little tricky. Of course my husband was privy to all of it; it's always a good idea to keep your Knight in Shining Armor in the loop. Still, the details of my little saga had not been approved for general audiences. Oh, no. And even for the purposes of this little story I've had to incorporate a five-second delay of sorts and about a million bleeps. Besides, I live in a small town. No one else needed to be burned by Anita's recklessness. Maybe it could end with me.

Maybe, kinda sorta.

The following Tuesday, during an exercise class that I teach, I found myself blurting out, "You know, I'm not as nice as I think I am!" after the class let out a collective, good-natured moan, when I instructed them to go to their mats for pushups. They hate push-ups. But they love me. And, of course, I had to explain. Kinda sorta.

When I told them about the text—even leaving out all the juicy parts and the identity of the hater—they were already suiting up to go to war with me. But their weapons were soft. No pointed poison darts. No retaliatory missiles. No, it was like a pillow fight. Lots of goofy energy and laughter and nobody gets hurt.

And now, everyone I know, *everyone*, has been warned. *I'm not as nice as I think I am.* If I asked Ted to put his dishes in the dishwasher—*You know, Sharla, you're not as nice as you think you are.* If I needed Taylor to move his car too early in the morning—*Mom, you're not as nice as you think you are.* If I forgot to call Kelly back—*Girl, you're not as nice as you think you are.* It was kind of a relief, actually. How nice do I need to be to redeem myself with the girl behind the curtain? Who knows? I'll keep trying. It's a worthy endeavor.

It's looking pretty good for me, however. As soon as I could muster the courage to expose my wounds to those who love me, the whole thing immediately began to scab over. It began to morph from tragedy to comedy. Santa Claus had the final word.

Our annual, crazy, family Christmas card set things straight once and for all. Every year for 22 years now we have designed and produced (with the help of my artist brother) original, off-the-wall, family photos or illustrations to send out to friends and relatives during the holidays. The year of Hurricane Ivan, the four of us were depicted—with a little help from Photoshop—blown sideways clinging to a palm tree. The Deepwater Horizon oil spill of 2010 inspired a family photo of the four of us, posing happily on the beach in matching khaki's and white polo shirts—covered in Hershey's chocolate syrup. In 2008 we were trapped, frantic, yet festive, in a giant snow globe. Back in 1996 we were caricatured playing volley ball with a bunch of snowmen on the beach. In 2014 we were stuffed into Christmas stockings and hung by the chimney with care. In 2000 we actually stripped down to our skivvies, and were photographed laying on the beach with sand covering our privates, to wish everyone a "Happy Nude Year."

The year of the *I'm not-as-nice-as-I-think-I-am* conundrum, we decided to let Saint Nick himself have a say. The illustration showed us as Christmas cookies on a platter awaiting the arrival of Santa, our terrified faces superimposed over cartoon gingerbread men, as our dog, Shuba, took a big chunk out of me.

On the inside of the card was Santa's checklist—from his official Naughty or Nice spreadsheet. And there, as plain as day, checkmarks in the NICE column for Ted, Myles, Taylor, *and* Sharla. (Alas, Shuba came up *naughty*). And here's the best part! Penciled in, in red, was the word, VERY, next to my NICE box. *VERY!* That settles it. Santa, himself, has spoken. And it turns out that I am not just nice. I'm *very* nice.

To be honest, many others have weighed in as well. In fact, everyone who loves me. Kelly even had stationery made for me that shamelessly declares, "Why yes, I *am* as nice as I think I am." I'm sure there will be a T-shirt before it's all over. And maybe a jingle. Maybe a smiling, bobble-headed Sharla, inscribed. And if I were to die tomorrow, I can't help but imagine my headstone:

Here lies Sharla, who was even nicer than she thought she was.

And for that legacy, I am grateful. Thank you, Anita. I was a mean girl once, too. I grew up. Maybe you will, too.

Schizophrenic Sky

Today, I am starting my work day early—and in a different "office." The morning is just too glorious to spend between four walls.

The sky is so full and layered and schizophrenic. I don't know whether to put on a bikini or a raincoat or Jenna's sweatpants.

To the south: along the smudged horizon, a flat-bottomed mountain range of billows presses *down* in charcoal curtains of rain showers far out over the Gulf, and *up* in stratums and wisps of dissipating clouds on high.

To the east: flannel gray storm clouds reach up with white lacy edges to blue-eye sky. So coarse and dense at the bottom and delicate at the top. Pretty.

To the west: a twenty layer cake, like my Aunt Loreen used to make, iced with reflected morning light. Above the frosted clouds, there is a tease of a sunny day—lavender bleeding up to blue again.

Everywhere I look is another possibility for this day. I don't get to choose it, though.

This cool north breeze could swing around and become heavy and hot with southern rain. The sun—where is the sun?—could blaze its way through the eastern cloud bank and burn things up like yesterday. Any one of the drapes of showers I see far out over the Gulf, could press toward shore and drench the beach, the walkover and me. The forecast is 50/50 for rain—a "meh" type of prediction. Maybe it'll rain on me—maybe it won't.

And I am fine with my indisputable powerlessness over the weather, because it has always been thus. I have learned to love the mystery of it, dark or bright, and I can relax into the uncertainty of the sky. I can let it be and not exert a single breath of effort, physical, emotional, or spiritual, in trying to manipulate all of the elements—horizon, cloud, sun and moon, showers, bird and breeze—that makes it a sky. How foolish would that be?

And now …

Big blops of rain splash onto my paper, and I'm chased inside if I want to continue putting pencil to page. But it will pass, probably in mere minutes, and some new thing will happen to the morning.

And I will adapt and participate and not begrudge the sky for being sky.

I am in conflict with someone I love. That southern sky, dark and foreboding. It is a hard relationship. I begrudge that sky. I am trying so hard not to, but I feel threatened and small, and wish I could change it with some of my light, so that I wouldn't feel afraid. So that it wouldn't hurt like it does.

But my light seems to be an annoyance. Some people just prefer the overcast—the threat of dangerous weather. They are scared too, I think. But it is what they know. It is what they create.

And I have a friend. Or had one. I really don't even know the proper tense. For a long time now, she has had no time for us. No space for me at all, and it is taking me a while to let that be okay. That eastern sky is beautiful and complicated and cluttered, and it seems that even a single bird could crash it all. I do not want to be that little gull.

I've been watching that sky for a couple of years now, waiting patiently for a clearing, a small space for lunch maybe, or a walk on the beach. And it clears a little from time to time, as all skies do, but rarely for me. I try not to be sad about it; even good friendships run out of sky.

The time for imposing my elements, be they pelicans or rainbows, lightning spears or hurricanes, has passed. We had many good and loving seasons. I am grateful for that. Still, I miss that sky. It was my favorite.

And my Jenna. That western sky of everything at once. How can it be that she is nowhere in body yet everywhere in soul? Everything about her, I miss. My niece, my friend, so lovely and deep and magnificent. That sky reaching up and across to a clear place of soft light and peace. Still, I want to hear her laugh just once more. To be sure that she's okay. That's all, just to be sure.

But there's nothing sure about the sky except change. Still, I see that the higher I set my gaze, the clearer it gets.

A few weeks ago, I lay on my back on the warm, flat rocks at Diamond Lake with a different niece. Above us floated a single fat cloud. Dana said, "Watch it disappear."

We lay there, barely blinking, and the cloud simply dissolved into the stark blue sky before our eyes. It was freaky.

That happens. Things change. Sometimes they dissolve while you're watching or go away forever while you're not. Sometimes they mess with your mind. Sometimes it's not the sky in the travel brochure, the sky you thought you paid good money for. And sometimes it's so beautiful anyway it takes your breath away.

And sometimes it's a schizophrenic sky. And you pack accordingly.

Sharla Dawn Gorder

....

Redemption

Surge

The birds are especially noisy this morning, and I like that. I've been observing them for weeks now. They fascinate me. They inspire me. *Do they know that they're endangered? Is that why they're so determined?*

They are nesting on the beach behind the house. I mean, right there on the wide-open beach, depositing their eggs in a small divot in the sand. No twigs and moss and feathers formed into a bowl to cradle their hatchlings. No sheltering tree limbs to conceal their incubating progeny. Just a "scrape" in the stark sand. Their vulnerability is alarming. Two different species of birds are nesting together, the sleek and elegant Black Skimmer in their tiny tuxedos, and the Least Tern, one of the smallest of the gull family. The Florida Wildlife Conservation Commission has cordoned off the area, but the birds themselves do a damn good job of keeping inquisitive tourists away from their babies.

I pass within a couple hundred feet of their nesting area on my afternoon walks. They circle and screech, then dive bomb into my hair. And though each bird alone is no bigger than a Snickers bar, together, they intimidate the hell out of me. I'm curious about their eggs, but don't even *consider* venturing close enough to gawk. *Mission accomplished, indefatigable little birds. I admire your dauntlessness.*

Yes, they are noisy this morning. Nonetheless, I will be sad in just a few weeks when they migrate southward with their fledglings. They make me feel hopeful somehow, persevering as they do against all odds. They make me think of Emily Dickinson's poem:

Hope is the thing with feathers
That perches in the soul
And sings the tune without the words
And never stops at all.

Hope, a tireless shorebird carrying the tune of life even when I've grown too tired, or too stubborn, or too lazy, or simply too bewildered, to sing it myself. Hope can always be found if I'm still enough, open enough. The little bird "never stops at all."

But there was a time when grief deafened me. It's like that awful, awful stillness the first morning after a hurricane—silence that feels dreadful, when the birds and the frogs and the crickets and even the winds are muted, and the absence of sound is eerie and unnatural.

Jenna, my golden niece, my cherished friend, had died. Suddenly, senselessly, in a freak accident. How could that possibly be? *How?* It just couldn't be true. She had turned 27 on Monday. I had mailed her a birthday present, money for a ticket home. I will wake up in just a minute, and she'll be back, sashaying down the beach like the she-sells-seashells-on-the-seashore girl. Seashore girls do not drown. No. no. Please, *no*. Are you there, God? Straighten this all out, please.

He did not straighten it all out. At least not to my liking.

I wept and slept and drank—just to weep and sleep and drink some more. I stood knee deep in the churning surf and raged at God on the shore of the very beach Jenna haunted. Until I could rage no more. And the quiet, the hideous quiet, engulfed me like hurricane surge, and I was lost to myself.

My best friend at that time, Vanessa, could see that the silence, the grief of my sudden and tragic loss was killing me, and it broke her heart to see me suffering so. Vanessa became that *thing with feathers* and nested right there in my soul, and stayed there with me until I could hear the songbird again.

She did this, among many ways, through quotes. Vanessa was not a reader, certainly not a writer, but she knew that *I* was both and that the written word was very meaningful to me. So every single day, she "serenaded" me with words. Every morning, I would wake up swollen-eyed and mournful, to a text on my phone:

> *August 3: "There is no despair so absolute as that which comes with the first moments of our first great sorrow, when we have not yet known what it is to have suffered and be healed, to have despaired and recovered hope."*
> *George Elliot*
> *September 5: "The deeper that sorrow carves into your being, the more joy you can contain." Khalil Gibran*
> *October 9: "I find hope in the darkest of days, and focus in the brightest. I do not judge the universe." Dalai Lama*

Day after day, week after week, Vanessa faithfully sent the quotes, and gradually I began hearing again the gentle trilling of the feathered thing, the resurgence of hope.

> *November 14: "Friendship improves happiness and abates misery, by the doubling of our joy and the dividing of our grief." Cicero*
> *November 23: "Grief can be the garden of compassion. If you keep your heart open through everything, your pain*

*can become your greatest ally in our life's search for love
and wisdom." Rumi*

*December 12: "Weeping may endure for a night but joy
cometh in the morning." God*

On December 19th, after 150 days of texting me these healing words, Vanessa sent this powerful quote by one of my favorite writers, Ann Lamott:

> **"You will lose someone you cannot live without,** *and
> your heart will be badly broken, and the bad news is that
> you never completely get over the loss of your beloved. But
> this is also the good news. They live forever in your broken
> heart that doesn't seal back up. And you come through.
> It's like having a broken leg that never heals perfectly—
> that still hurts when the weather gets cold, but you learn
> to dance with the limp."*

Four days after she sent this text, Vanessa died suddenly.

But *the thing with feathers* lived on. Somehow, some way, the hope that Vanessa had rekindled in me didn't die with her. I am so grateful to her for that.

Did she know that she was endangered? Is that why she was so determined?

I spoke at Vanessa's memorial, and every head nodded when I said that she was the president of everyone's fan club. It didn't take a tragedy to garner her encouragement. I had written in my journal a few years back when struggling with depression: "Vanessa is my biggest fan. She buoys me up when I get heavy. She makes me laugh. She fills out the baggy edges of my personality. She loves out loud. (She does everything out loud.)"

And you'd think that death—as powerful as it is, as cunning and cruel as it seems—would silence even the most robust of cheerleaders. But Vanessa's humble gift of words, of carefully chosen inspiration, lived on with me even after her soul had departed. I carried them—texted to my phone, written in my journal, and imprinted on my heart. She changed me, and unwittingly prepared me for her own death. *You will lose someone you cannot live without …*

And what she did was not Hollywood heroic—she didn't rescue me from vampires or intercept a bullet on the battlefield or offer up one of her kidneys for me. But she saved me nonetheless.

Very simply, with care and determination, without fanfare and self-promotion, she encouraged me. Every single day until she died. She encouraged me.

And this, I believe now more than ever in my life, is what we must do for each other. It doesn't have to be with quotes, or grand gestures of charity, or inspiring sermons or stories, or anything contrived or highfalutin. We simply must *encourage each other.* We must make it a habit to validate others, to *refrain from disparaging* anyone, anywhere. That includes our spouses and our children. But also, co-workers, family members, even strangers we encounter along the way. And of course, our best friends. We have no idea how much time we have left. I would have liked four more *decades* with Vanessa. Four days is what I got.

I've always sensed, ever since I was a little kid, that this is my *raison d'être*—the reason I'm here—to encourage, maybe even inspire. That said, I fall so short every single day. My ego gets in the way. My insecurities. My fear. So many days I am petty and vain. But some days I get it right.

I keep a note on my desk next to my computer where I do my writing. My son wrote it on an index card in purple sharpie a couple of years ago. He wrote it for me.

You inspire happiness … no trait is even comparable.

And that may be my favorite quote of all. Simple words of encouragement and affirmation from a teenage boy to his mom. Eight words. They inspire me to do better, to *be* better every single day. He probably doesn't even remember writing them. And even though I believe that *he* is the one with the gift of inspiring happiness, I will strive to be the person he believes me to be, because, I agree—*no trait is even comparable.*

Vanessa had an intuitive knowledge of this, and she was brave and tireless and determined. And I survived, Vanessa. I thrived.

Mission accomplished, indefatigable little bird. I admire your dauntlessness.

Morning Mourning

I pulled the lawn chair around to face the rising sun and pulled the zipper up on my first sweatshirt of the season. I'm wearing sweatpants, too—Jenna's soft gray ones. They're about half-a-foot too long for me, but they're Jenna's. I wish I could remember seeing her in them. Ah, always I wish I could remember things about Jenna—anything. Everything. I suspect that "time healing all wounds" is due, at least in part, to the fading of memories. If that is the case, then let my wound stay open and bleeding. I'd rather remember her and bleed than forget her and heal. Healing is a little rushed and over-rated, I think.

I love morning shadows in the sand. Every footprint is visible when the sun is low. Even the seaoats throw their slender shadows down in stark stripes across the dune. The old wooden walkover makes me feel hopeful somehow, starting in the sand *here* and ending in the sand *there*—spanning not water, as piers do, but more of the same: sand. Point A is point B, as is the rickety line that connects them. All the same. The past is the future is the present. All one.

I'm happy about this new north wind. It charms all of my senses at once. It even cools my coffee just enough to drink right now; I don't have to wait. It mellows the heat of this celebrated Florida sunshine on my face. It tames the sea and sharpens the horizon line, which seems to be everywhere and nowhere all at once. And again, I feel hopeful about that. The Gulf makes no sound this morning, but the palm trees are noisy.

I am hopeful. And I am hurting. I never got to say goodbye to her, which seems abrupt and tragic—even as I stumble through this *next* sad but *drawn-out* goodbye at my *mom's* bedside, holding her impossibly tiny hand, kissing her soft white hair—just at the temple where, if I'm very still, my lips can feel a small pulse. For how much longer, I cannot know.

I miss them both so acutely. No one can tell me how to do this, least of all my mother. Her telling days are gone now, used up by time and love and dementia, and all of those things that make up a very long life. Too long? I wonder. Is it meant to go on like this, so long after all the pleasure is gone?

Certainly this *long goodbye* is better than that *no goodbye*. Either way, it's hard. Ted says I need to learn to compartmentalize. But everything on my plate touches. And is there a compartment big enough to hold the one who knew me before I even knew myself, the one I've known from the very inside of her being? I read some beautiful words from a mother to her child: *No one else will ever know the strength of my love for you. After all, you're the only one who knows what my heart sounds like from the inside.*

I remember, Mom. I think I do. But I will let you go. I will. I will let that beat tap down to silence when it's time. It is the least I can do. It is the most I can do.

And I will heal. Or I won't. But I will always remember. There will never be a compartment for you, Mom. Just as there will never be one for Jenna. You are both, point A and B, and the rickety line between for me.

Do Tell

I'm just the teensiest bit compulsive (and prone to understatement). I have been this way for as long as I can remember. I like to think I'm just a little quirky, so that I don't have to think that I'm just a little crazy. They say there's a genetic component to OCD (Thanks, Mom) and that it dovetails nicely with all kinds of other disorders, afflictions and addictions. You don't have to be a mental health professional to see the connection. No, you could follow me around for a few decades and get a pretty good idea of how this works. Don't have time for that? Well, let me break it down for you:

- I once gathered up every white sock in the entire house—even Taylor's itty bitty ones the size of cashews—and threw them all in the garbage with coffee grounds dumped on top, and went to Target and bought brand new ones for everybody, because I couldn't bear the sight of even one more mate-less sock in the laundry.

- I carefully alphabetized all of my spices and turned all labels to face east (toward Mecca?) because no one needs three cream of tartars and four corianders. And now that I could see what I had, maybe I wouldn't buy a fifth paprika.

- I ate nine "Hot, Now!" Krispy Kreme donuts alone in my car in the 20 minutes it took me to drive from Destin to Mary Esther. And tossed the last three, along with the box, into a dumpster behind 7/11, because well, inquiring minds would want to know—and I didn't want them to.

- I suddenly found myself jogging on the utility strip of an interstate outside Tokyo because, in my head, I still had twelve more minutes to run before I was allowed to double back toward the hotel. Never mind, though. The Japanese highway patrol thought it best I cut my run short, and they escorted me back in a car with bars and brightly flashing lights.

- I drank eight Cosmopolitans one night during a girls' weekend getaway and threw up seven of them into my own purse because Tammy's brand-new Suburban still had that new car smell, and it was so clean, and maybe no one would notice. (Uh, they noticed.)

- I rewrote, four times, this quote to put on my refrigerator, because the "P" should have been capitalized, or my handwriting looked sloppy, or it needed to be centered: *Perfection is the enemy of done.*

- I watched all 210 episodes of Everybody Loves Raymond, in less than a month because I had been feeling depressed, and everybody knows that laughter is the best medicine, and I was out of Zoloft.

- I flossed my teeth three times in a row, one right after the other, because I had skipped two days and had to make up for it to get back on track.

- I straightened the crooked painting at Lillo's, our favorite Italian restaurant—just the one in my line of sight—even though I knew it was intentionally hung askew for design purposes—because I couldn't eat my chicken parmesan with that thing all cattywampus in my face.

- I decided to go on a diet. I'd start it on Monday, as all diets must start on Monday. And wouldn't it be better to start it on the first Monday of the month. Or better yet, Monday, the first of the year. Yes, that is the most auspicious of diet-starting dates: The first Monday of the first day of the year. I'll pencil that in—January 1st, 2018. And if that doesn't stick, there's another one right around the corner, in 2029.

- I banned all Christmas presents not wrapped in color-coordinated wrapping paper, from being placed beneath my turquoise, silver, and white-themed tree. I was visibly shaken when a dinner guest placed his sneaky Santa gift, wrapped in red, black and white paper, front and center. Did he not get the memo?

- I counted every step, in sets of four, that I took on my hour-long runs around the Sydney Opera House and Botanical Gardens. I counted the steps from the back door of my house to the Gulf (310), my bedroom to my office (29), and my car to the door of the gym (46-63, depending on my parking karma.)

- I carried a single paper clip I had found on the floor around with me for three hours while facilitating a medical conference. I had no pockets, and the appropriate paper clip place was on my registration table back in the conference room and I couldn't just throw it away; that would be wasteful.

- I read the entire users' manual cover to cover when I bought my first car—with little checkmarks in the corner of each page to keep me honest. I particularly enjoyed reading about the viscosity classes of engine oils, the California Emission Control System Limited Warranty

Parts List and the implied warranty of merchantability, which is, of course, limited to the duration of the express warranties herein.

- I added four items to my daily to-do list that I had already done because, well, I *had* done them, and I'd be damned if I wasn't gonna get credit. Besides, the list is so much more impressive to look at with lots and lots of line items with lots and lots of strikethroughs. Too much empty space on any calendar page implies that I'm a slacker. Which I, most certainly, am not!

- And then there was that time when I was a teenager and decided that food was highly overrated, and maybe I could avoid it altogether if instead of actually eating it, I obsessed about eating it every moment I was conscious and many moments I was not, thereby slowly starving myself.

- And then, decades later, I decided that alcohol was highly underrated, and maybe I could get away with drinking it continuously instead of moderately, every day for a very long time, thereby slowly annihilating myself.

Oh dear. This is the part where I talk about those specific Colliding Vices that must be "acknowledged, eradicated and atoned for." How easy, it seems, for a funny little quirk to morph into a pathological obsession. How quickly, it seems, a familiar comfort zone can transform into a deadly danger zone.

In truth, though, it is rarely easy or quick—this descent into the madness of anorexia or addiction. It takes discipline and perseverance to get there. In fact, it uses up both of those qualities in the most subversive of ways until you are left with neither to help you escape. No self-control. No purpose. No way out, it seems.

I have been on my knees in my dark bedroom in both scenarios whimpering, "God, why won't you help me?" Silence. Seems he wouldn't tell me why. He wouldn't tell me anything, or maybe he tried—but I couldn't hear his voice, the voice of reason and of grace, for the din of disordered thinking that had highjacked my brain, my body, my soul. In both cases, I was trudging, or staggering along on a slow, hungry death march. I didn't want to die. But being alive didn't seem to be working for me, either.

And yes, it's all a learning process—if you don't go ahead and die. Sometimes you do; I know that now. I've seen it happen. But having been spared myself, I can say that the biggest lesson I've learned is this: the way it *seems* when gripped by an obsession is not the way it *is*. *God, that is so important.* But you couldn't have told me that—as a teenager when I was congratulating myself for my willpower and discipline on the days when I consumed fewer than 500 calories, subsisting on iceberg lettuce, yellow mustard, and Premium Saltine Crackers. You couldn't have told me that—as an adult when I was positive that the only relief from my excruciating anxiety and grief was an ice-cold Pinot Grigio, at 10:15 in the morning. These compulsions were the *solutions* to my problems, or so it seemed. And though my problems were real—whether genetically imposed, as anxiety and depression often are, or imposed by life, as disappointment and death always are—the relief I was seeking could not be found in my refrigerator. I know. I looked.

I have learned that when you're suffering—either acutely as in the stunning horror of sudden loss, or chronically, as with severe depression or anxiety—relief is all you crave. And there comes a point that any respite will do, no matter the cost. It will cost a lot. But you will ignore your mounting psychic debt for absolutely as long as you can, because, in the moment, the cool rim of that first glass against your lips reminds you that there is a different way to feel; it gives you hope, maybe. And then a few gulps later you're left staring at the bottom of your glass. And the bottom of the glass is just not bearable, so you pour it in till it brims. And *again* and then maybe just once or twice more so you can sleep. And you forget your pain for a very short while, but you also forget your dreams. When did it become a matter of just getting through the day until you could be unconscious again?

But sleep is fitful and tenuous and morning comes like mourning—and it breaks your heart to awaken. And the cycle repeats and repeats and repeats, and the shame of it all shoves you deeper and deeper into solitary confinement in a prison of your own creation, and even your hour in the yard becomes intolerable. You beg to be left alone.

Just leave me alone, Mom. Can't you see I just need to lose three more pounds? Just leave me alone, Ted. Don't you understand that I need this glass of wine? I need it just to feel normal; I'm not having a party here. Just leave me alone. I've got this under control.

Control. Cliché but true. I need to feel like this is all controllable and that I get to hold the remote. Every compulsion I indulge, from benign teeth-flossing to malignant calorie-counting to the deadly metastasis of addiction, is a grab for the clicker. But soon the batteries are dead, and those buttons I've always pressed to change the channel on my mood don't work anymore. Hopelessness sets in. Which forebodes the end—or heralds a beginning. Your choice.

My choice. I always had choices. At 15, at 35, at 50. Now. There is always some alternative. But isolation and shame were hard crusts that formed over the top of possibility, and the obsessive brain that brought me to this place on my knees railing at a god I no longer liked, that mind had been struck deaf, dumb and blind to possibility. Einstein said, "We cannot solve our problems with the same thinking we used when we created them."

Of course we can't. If we could've, we would've. If it were as simple as saying, "Ah, I'm not eating enough to sustain my life. I think I'll go eat a sandwich now." Or, "Wow, I don't remember going to bed again last night, I think I'll quit drinking today." If it were that simple, we would all be hunky-dory.

It isn't. We're not. My brain told me that my life was better this way—actually, that it was the only way. Even as a skeletal teenager who saw black every time she stood up. Even as a middle-aged mom who, in the end, would wake up, from hell-dreams, shaking, craving, dying. My thinking—the thinking that delivered me to my nightmares, could not save me.

So then, what could? What would? What did?

You did. Yes, you. You, my son. You, my mother. You, my spouse. You, my best friend. You, the toll booth operator. You, the guy at CVS. You, my ladies at the gym. You, the toddler across the street. You, the addict in the rooms. You, my creator. You, the dog at my feet. You, the songwriter. You, the artist. You, the yoga instructor. You, the aunt. You, the niece. You. All of you.

But I had to let you. And to let you, I had to connect with you in some way. I had written in my journal during my darkest time: "Disconnection is fatal—taken to the extreme edge, as in addiction, depression, madness. Detachment always ends in the death of something. Sometimes, the death of everything." To *live*, I needed to go sit next to you, be with you and your friends, your family. I don't even like the term "reach out" because the metaphor implies too much effort, athletic and purposeful, and my soul was neither; it took all of the energy I had, simply to look up from my life. But when I finally did, I saw you.

And I introduced myself, as if for the first time. And you smiled back, and invited me to sit at your table, or swim in your pool, or play in your yard. And in a little time, we talked. I told you things. You told me your things. And that was a start. I learned that you have been lost, too. Maybe not in the same jungle or swamp or bottomless ocean, but you, too, have struggled. *You, too, have struggled.* It's not just me. St. Therese de Avilar wrote: "To reach something good, it is very useful to have gone astray and thus acquire experience." Your experience can help me. And, how fortuitous is this? Mine can help you. But you have to talk to me. I have to talk to you.

I am convinced that while many, many factors contribute to my waywardness during difficult times in my life, the one that keeps me lost and in peril is shame. Researcher Brené Brown, writes, "Shame needs three things to grow out of control in our lives: secrecy, silence, and judgment." I know this to be true.

And though it can be scary at first letting those feral cats out of their bags—*What have I done?*—you will find that they are far less vicious in the light of day than in the dark litter box of your mind, where they can claw your eyes out from the inside. At least, when you let them out, they have the savage beasts of others to play with.

I told. Just one person, to start. Just one person I trusted. I told Ted. And with that one confession, that one plea for help, my shame no longer had what it needed to fester. My "*secret*" was out. My deadly *silence* was broken. And as my shame began to diminish, so did my brutal self-judgment, along with my fear that *others* would judge me harshly. It helped that not only did Ted refuse to *judge* me, he *joined* me in the fray. From the very first day. Seemed he'd been waging his own private battle with the bottle, too. I had been too soul-sick to see. So we held hands. That's the best way to do scary things. It's one of the rules Robert Fulghum reminds us of in his list of things he learned in Kindergarten: When you go out into the world, watch out for traffic, hold hands, and stick together.

Why didn't I remember this? Why did I suffer in silence for so long? Why do you?

I don't know you, or maybe I do, but I do know this: The next time you find yourself in that black, bleak pre-dawn hour—suddenly, regrettably conscious, with dread and remorse sucking you down, down, down, like quicksand—the next time you awaken and wish you hadn't because it's just too hard, remember this: It doesn't have to be this way. It doesn't.

Talk to someone. A real person. Talk to your best friend, your rabbi or minister, your aunt or your cousin. Hell, talk to that toll booth operator. Tell them about the paper-clip place and the alphabetized spices and have a good laugh. But tell them, when it's time, about the deadly hunger, or the drowning thirst as well, and have a good cry. But tell.

Do tell.

All Told

So I told. And not just God this time. I told Ted. You'd think I wouldn't have to tell on myself, that it would be obvious to everyone—that there would be a whole committee of interventionists ready to swoop in and rescue me. But this wasn't my case. I was dangerously discreet in my battle, but my very soul was dying. And since no one had ever had to scrape me off of a barroom floor, or bail me out of jail, or even take away my car keys, I didn't show up on Dr. Drew's radar. No one knew the awful truth. Not even my husband.

Not even myself. I knew I was messed up—this time in a perilous, imminently deadly way—but even I couldn't separate the crushing grief over Jenna's death, the ensuing depression, the life-long undercurrent of acute anxiety, and my myriad compulsions. It was all a black blur.

And getting blacker by the day. I had tried everything but one thing. Told my doctors everything but one thing. Blamed everything but one thing.

I blamed my genes. My mom suffered from severe depression and anxiety much of her life, as did her mother. Mom went to bed in her fifties and didn't feel much like getting up ever again.

I blamed grief. I had never experienced the full force of it before. Losing Jenna felt like losing the stars. The heavens went dark.

I blamed my own personality. *This is just the way I am. I've always been this way. People don't change.*

And finally, I blamed God. I clearly remember being on my knees in my dim bedroom, whimpering, "Where are you, God?"

But when I wrapped my fingers around the cold stem of that wineglass at 10:30 in the morning on a Monday, something shifted. I can't tell you why it was this particular morning and not any number of equally bleak moments, but that morning I clutched that glass in my hand and slid down the kitchen cabinets to the floor. I drank it. And I was done. *This* was that one thing.

I called Ted at work. He came home. We made a plan.

It started, as most plans do, with a decision. I love Augusten Burroughs' take on it: "Decisions are beautiful. They are the polishing cloths of life." And while this one specific decision didn't eradicate all of my dysfunctional pathology, psychology and theology in one fell swoop, it did begin that polishing process that changed every single aspect of my life for the better. There is no part of my life that wasn't positively affected by the decision to change this *one thing*.

One thing only that day. Ted and I stopped drinking alcohol on the same day several years ago.

To say that this abrupt withdrawal almost killed me is not hyperbole. Around the third day I was so sick, I sought medical help. Around the third week, the fog started to lift. Around the third year, I went to my doctor for a routine physical. I had absolutely nothing to write in the space that used to be too small to list all of my medications and substances. I did tell him that I still run with scissors on occasion.

It was hard. But it isn't hard now. And even if it was, I know now that I can do hard things. It seems so odd to me now that not drinking alcohol seemed like such an absurd proposition. I remember listening to a guy struggling with his own alcoholism as he described his reluctance to give it up once and for all. He just couldn't stand the thought of not being able to share a champagne toast at his daughter's wedding. His daughter was *two* at the time of his admission. I could relate. The thought of never drinking alcohol again made me feel somehow lonely and oddballish. I had never even tried to quit before—mostly because I thought I could not do it. Since my first piña colada at a house party in East Hill when I was a teenager, to my final greedy gulp of Pinot Grigio on the floor of my kitchen, I had always been a drinker, with brief breaks for pregnancies and nursing. It didn't concern me—until it did. I hadn't always imbibed in my bathrobe and socks alone on the cold tile. That was a relatively new development. I drank like everyone else. Until I didn't.

And I do not know when I crossed that line. I love the descending elevator analogy I've often heard. My elevator opened to many, many floors between the time I first found myself as a young mom thinking, "It's been a rough day, I *deserve* a glass of wine," to the desperate morning years later when I found myself picking at crumbs on the floor by the refrigerator, my first drink of the day in my hand—at 10:30 AM. I could have gotten off at, "OMG, that was fun, but this hangover is pure hell." Or, "Oh, shit, did I really text that last night?" Or finally, "I wonder how it'd feel to add a couple of Xanax to the mix." That floor should have killed me.

It didn't. See, it *didn't*. I am so very not dead. I am more alive than I ever dreamt I could be. Certainly more than I *should* be. I wake up every morning without shame. That, to me, is the best part. Life is still really, really hard sometimes—surely never more so than during these last couple of years of heartbreaking loss. But sadness, even excruciating grief, is endurable with a clear mind—and a clear conscience. Once I gave up on the notion that some substance or compulsive behavior would help me cope, I was free to live my life according to values that, despite my waywardness, had always been an intrinsic part of me. I was no longer flailing against myself. My behavior started to line up with my ethics. And that was so freeing.

In the beginning, when people would ask me why I wasn't drinking at social events, I'd laugh and say, "I'm not thirsty anymore." Then I'd tell them my simple truth: I lost the privilege. I was drinking irresponsibly and pathologically. I couldn't handle alcohol anymore, so I quit. Invariably, they'd ask, "For how long? Like a month or a year?" And I'd tell them another of my simple truths: "*Forever.*" I will never be able to handle alcohol. That ship sailed many hangovers ago. And I'm fine with that—a little relieved, actually. One less daily decision to make. I can't have and do every single thing on the planet. And taking away alcohol wasn't the tragedy I imagined it might be. Quite the opposite. I have so much more to celebrate—and I get to *remember* it all— without a headache. Without regret.

People were curious. And just a few months into my recovery, the "why" questions morphed into the much more complicated "how" inquiries. I wasn't the only one in my social circle who was struggling. That became tragically evident to me just a few weeks sober, when a dear friend's elevator opened for the last time at the very bottom, and she died drunk.

I would like to say that once I made my decision, I simply pulled myself up by my bootstraps, or bathrobe sash, and carried on triumphantly. But it didn't happen that way. No, not at all.

Ted was able to do it that way, but not me.

Once I made the *one* decision to stop drinking alcohol, just the *one*, (I didn't decide to overhaul my whole life there from the floor of my kitchen, I just decided to quit drinking) I solicited help from every source available. I knew, intuitively, that I could not solve this problem alone. I had failed so many times to simply *moderate* my drinking; I'd never be able to quit this habit without a lot of support.

I had never done this before. Never *seen* it done before. I don't come from a long line of alcoholics and addicts. Neither of my parents drank a drop when I was growing up. Nor did aunts, uncles or grandparents, at least not in my presence. I had no experience with "recovery" or "sobriety" or "one day at time-ing" or any of the other buzzwordy aspects of this path I had chosen. But I chose it nonetheless. I would say I had no choice. But the truth is that my elevator had quite a few more increasingly pernicious floors to descend to before it bottomed out.

But I was afraid of the basement. Despite the seemingly reckless behavior that delivered me to the cold floor of my kitchen, I'm not an impulsive person. I'm not the chick in the horror flick that's compelled to explore the cellar when things go bump in the night. Oh, no. Thank God. Literally, *God thank you*, for instilling in me a healthy fear of the basement. Basements are dark and dank and dangerous—and, most tragically, uninhabited, except maybe by monsters or psychopaths, or that tall, faceless guy in a black robe and hood brandishing a scythe.

No, I got off on a floor that was still doing business. Ted was there. Kitty, a wise and compassionate counselor, had an office there. The welcoming fellowship of AA was there. A music room was there. A whole library of inspirational books was there. The exercise class I teach was there. My BFF was there. A tranquil yoga studio was there. The beach was there. A fresh supply of Paper Mate Sharp Writer #2 mechanical pencils was there. God was there.

I got off on *that* floor. I stepped out and the elevator doors shut behind me. I still had to go *knocking* on all those doors, and that took all the humility and courage I could muster, but knock, I did, and every single door opened graciously to me, as messed up as I was. No one turned me away. I am so grateful.

Yesterday was Thanksgiving. I entertained a crowd of dear family and friends, and it was my pleasure and privilege to carve the turkey and whisk the gravy and even pour the wine. (I don't presume to know what floor anyone else is on or even if they're in that building.) I pulled the biscuits out of the oven and looked around the crowded kitchen—happy, hungry people hovering over this feast that we had prepared together, eager to chow down. Gratitude overwhelmed me. I dropped the oven mitt and bent to pick it up off the floor. What a contrast, this kitchen floor with that one. I'm thankful for them both.

Today, at yoga, as we all returned to our mats for the final restorative pose—Savasana, or corpse pose—Sydney, my instructor said, "Welcome the floor."

I did. I do.

Dear James

This story is for James Taylor. So, if you are not James Taylor, you can skip this chapter and go on to the next chapter, "Six-pack."

If you *are* James Taylor, first of all, let me say that I, too, am very pleased to meet you. You may not remember, but when you shook my hand there over the chain-link fence at the Columbia Gorge in 1994, you did tell me you were pleased to meet me. I think you were sincere.

In fact, you always seem sincere to me, James—that's why I'm so fond of you. Whether you are a steamroller, a death-row inmate, a millworker's daughter, a chili dog, a bartender, a lighthouse, a frozen man, a Red Sox fan, a trucker, a drug dealer, a handyman or a golden retriever puppy dog, I believe you are the real thing. I have always believed this. And while I'm not saying you're a religion or anything (I'm not a lunatic), it has really helped me to believe in you all of these years.

I was twelve when we first met, and our relationship has outlasted every single nonfamilial bond I've had in my life. Why, today, we are even Facebook friends! I love the videos you post. Of course, back then, I only had the music. Oh, and the album cover. I worried that the needle on my hi-fi would wear out the record the way my hands were fraying the jacket. (Those solemn eyes. That chambray shirt.) But, like I said, it lasted. You lasted. And here we are, James.

Yes, it is now nearly half a century later, and you are still a daily part of my life. I could not write a book chronicling the major influences in my life without writing about my 45-year relationship with you. It has been profound, and not a day goes by that I don't consider something you have said in a song. Even messing with the thermostat yesterday, I was determined to cool my room to exactly 68 degrees. And I'm forever curious about what it is you have to show me in the garden. (I've imagined that it's a fragrant, fluffy peony, the size of a dinner plate, dusty pink and moonlit.) Last week, when I was making great progress organizing a story, I heard that gospel choir in my head, *In line, in line, it's all in line, my ducks are all in a row.* I woke up this morning singing, *Today, today, today, I'm finally on my way.* Thank you for hanging out with me every day, James.

I wonder how it must feel for you to read all of this. Is it weird? You mentioned that it is indeed curious when *perfect strangers call you by name.* I don't mean for this to be weird. But I have to tell you that when I made the decision to name my son Taylor James a couple of decades ago, I guess I felt comfortable enough with my commitment to you to know that we would stand the test of time. And we have.

But let me make this clear from the get-go: With the exception of a brief preadolescent crush in 1971, I have always kept it platonic. You recorded "You Can Close Your Eyes" that year, and it was the most romantic song I had ever heard. Who could resist such enchantment? To this day, every sunset I have ever witnessed has the same tender soundtrack. *And I still love you.* I know. I know—as I've heard you say in concert—"It helps that you don't know me." I get that. I'm not a stalker or anything, and besides, I was twelve-and-a-half. Anyway, it would be hard to be in love with a man with so many highway songs.

So, for the most part, the relationship I've imagined has been more the *James I'm wondering, could I borrow your truck?* variety. *That's why you're here.* You said it yourself. You have been a good friend. A very good friend. I have borrowed your truck countless times in my life. I would've been stranded on some very lonely roads without you.

I borrowed it when I was seventeen and decided to leave home and move to Costa Rica. I was *moving in silent desperation*, and it helped me to know that you were, too. I wasn't alone that summer or any season thereafter. *Winter, spring, summer or fall, all I had to do was call,* or listen. I borrowed it when I first saw my husband-to-be. There really was *something in the way he moved or looked my way or called my name.* You helped me to see it, to appreciate it. Even when, years later, I found I had forgotten how *to tend my own fire,* Ted was there, reaching down for me, saying, *Jump up behind me, my love. Jump up behind me.* To this day, he truly is *my only one only one.*

I borrowed your truck, James, when I was a new mother so very far from home, overwhelmed and lonely on *another gray morning, a not so good morning after all.* I was so desperately *locked up inside.* I borrowed it when I awoke angry or sad and beating myself up for waking angry or sad and finally accepting that sometimes *I can't help it if I don't feel so good. Everybody gets the blues. (Poor puppy.)* You helped me learn to give myself a break for a change, to try to live in the moment, and *make today, today.*

I borrow your truck when I grapple with all of my contradictions. Am I a *true believer, or a poor, wretched unbeliever?*

Do I need *a strong hit from the money machine*, or do I really not care *if I got no money (not a dime)*? Is love *just a word I've heard when things were being said*, or is it really *the only road*. I don't know any of those answers, don't understand the *why or when*, but you've assured me that *even in the middle of the sadness, this everyday madness*, there's a reason for it all—even when I just can't see it.

Though it was terrifying for me to finally acknowledge how far down I had plunged (so far down, James, so deep, *and the sides were pretty steep*), you taught me that if I would *just look up from my life*, I would see that I wasn't the first to find myself *knocking 'round the zoo*. It was even a Thursday. Seems I had forgotten how to be conscious comfortably, and finally, even *sleep could not free me*. I thought nothing could. I was wrong—you were right. Could you really *understand the girl that the monkey could leave behind?* And if *you* could, could others? Would there be grace for me? Was there, then, hope for *me*? You had been there, done that. You told me all about it. But it was so long ago for you. Still, I suspect that's one *mess of misery* you never forget. There were many angels, James, *watching over me*. You were one of them. You never stopped singing for me. And I agree, James, *there's only one way to surrender*. I get that now.

Thank you, James, for telling me your stories. They have changed me in ways great and small for most of my life. I will be borrowing your truck till I die. Even now, right this moment, as I'm feeling acutely overwhelmed and distraught over things I cannot control, I hear the soundtrack—those horns, James, the strings, those voices. *Seems I was born with too many choices. They confuse me. Really.* Those are my favorite lyrics, by the way. Ah, but you have inspired so many favorites of mine:

- Favorite colors: Deep greens and blues
- Favorite animal: Gorilla (*he's got hands on his feet!*)
- Favorite food: T-bone steak a-la-cartey
- Favorite ambient temperature: 68 degrees
- Favorite greeting: Boy howdy, howdy damn do!
- Favorite month: May
- Favorite dance: The cha-cha-cha
- Favorite highway song/mantra: *It's enough to be on my way.*

What relief, what joy to finally know that, yes, *it's enough to be on my way.* I'm *covering ground* every day. It's enough. And when I pray, James, I too *forget what to ask for. There really isn't anything I haven't been given.* Never mind *Armageddon and Waterloo.* Never mind *the zoo or the hole or the clock with no hands.* I have *this moment in the sun.* And it matters. *I'll plant my flag right here.*

You've been there through it all with me. Every milestone. Every crisis. Every celebration. For forty-five years. *We go on harmonizing a song.* There's always a song, James, always a song. You've been there, ready to lend me your truck—or maybe *your comb.*

And I've learned from you what a good and lovely and even *holy* thing it can be to *let the music change my mind.* I have been comforted, inspired and encouraged countless times by your voice, James, your strings, your words. I have also been made kinder by them. More humane.

In February, *the music changed my mind*—just in time maybe, or more likely (sadly), better late than never. But I saw it in Mom's eyes, James, there in her small dark eyes, so like the eyes of a child now—so earnest, though now rheumy with age and dementia and weariness. There it was, *that clock with no hands.* I hadn't wanted to see it. None of us did, but it had been there for years.

Is it odd that the death-row inmate in your song (the one that the State of Alabama incarcerated for murder) and my mom were both locked up by depression and madness and pled for the same thing? *Set me free. Sleep come free me. Please, please, please, set me free.*

Mom opened her eyes for a moment that winter afternoon. She had been mostly sleeping for a decade, maybe longer. Who could say where the depression left off, and the dementia took over? It was impossible to tell. Mom, never one to complain, retreated into her head and her bed. We could not rouse her. I even wrote her a song begging her to wake up—*You can't just fade away like this. Can't you hear your babies cry? We love you still, Mom, we always will. We can be your reasons why.*

But we couldn't. And those last months spent pressing a spoon to her lips, watching carefully, reminding her to swallow—the months of waking her up to have her diaper changed, of turning away from her because I could not watch (I *should* not watch)—the months of strumming music that she seemed not to hear, whispering stories that no longer resonated. Ah, those months.

I wanted her to wake up. To look at me. To tell me something witty, just one more time. We all did. We all wanted something from her. One more thing from Mom. Isn't that just the way with kids? We tried everything to rouse her back to life, back to us. But to be awake was torment for her. It *had* been for so very long. If language had not abandoned her, she would have said it too, "Sharshee, *It breaks my heart to awaken.*"

So, I let her sleep. Those final weeks, I *decided* to let her sleep. I put away the spoon and the straw that I had been using to drop water into her mouth, baby-bird style. I brought my guitar, my journal, a pillow from home.

I was with her when she fell asleep for the last time a few months ago, my strong body curled around her frail one, my lips whispering into her soft, white hair, "Go to sleep, Mom. It's okay. I understand. You can go now. You never have to face the heartbreak of awakening in this world again. I understand Mom, I do."

And she went. And she's gone.

And I'm okay, just *drifting through time and space on the face of this little blue ball falling around the sun* for a while longer. How much longer? No one knows.

But I do know the *Secret O' Life*, James. You confided in me, didn't you? Such a secret—so simple; and yet for *one who was lost and found, just like me and you*, so challenging.

Still, if *any fool can do it*, surely this one can.

Thanks, James. That's all I really mean to say. Thanks. I am forever in your debt, sir. With love. All the love that not knowing you allows. This is the epitome of unrequited, I suppose. But I'm okay with that.

This is a good love. One of the best loves of my life. Time and time again, *love has brought me around* through the music, and I see so clearly *how I'm gonna pay that debt I owe*. You're reading it. And with every word, every paragraph, every chapter, *I can feel it beginning to ease*.

Thanks, James.

Now about that truck …

God-ish

· · · · · · · ·

Six-pack

I'm not happy about this.

I bought a six-pack.

I hadn't gone to Target intending to buy a six-pack. No, I went to buy a rug for the kitchen. Nevertheless, I came home to my empty house (Ted was away fishing) with a six-pack (and no rug). I sat down with it, feeling sad and afraid, and wondered, how has it come to this?

I turned the package over in my hands and read the label— American Greetings, 6 Sympathy Cards, Stock up and Save!— and I realized, with dread, that I should have bought two six-packs. This wouldn't be enough.

The cards were very plain, in message and in design—clean, white background with a simple, blue doodle of flowery tendrils growing from the corners: *Wishing you peace. Wishing you healing. Wishing you hope.* And on the inside: *Wishing you everything your heart needs to get through this sad time. In sympathy.*

In addition to the six cards and envelopes, the package included an inventory card—a little chart with the words, *Sympathy cards sent,* at the top, and a bunch of lines below. My first thought was, *Is this for the aftermath of a plane crash, or a deadly apartment fire, or maybe a terrorist attack?* Who needs all that space to record the names of grieving friends and loved ones?

And then I acknowledged, *I* do. Sadly, *I* do. And no planes had gone down, no apartment buildings had gone up, and no ISIS attacks had gone on in my neighborhood. No, I needed all those cards and more, simply to keep up with regular old life—and death.

In the four months preceding this purchase, I had attended six funerals—four for elderly relatives and friends, one for a young man in his twenties, and one for a child. It seems that in the four *decades* preceding, I had barely been to that many. What's going on?

I sat down yesterday to begin writing in this fresh batch of cards, and the first four friends on my "list" were all grieving the loss of mothers. I understand this kind of sorrow. It is fresh for me. Still, as sincerely as I empathize and as much as I love words, I always stutter when it comes to expressing my condolences. No matter how much thought I put into them, words always seem so trite in the face of death. Milan Kundera spoke of the "vanity of words" and never do they seem more vain, than when trying to say something *meaningful* to someone who has just *lost* meaning—or at least the flesh and blood manifestation of meaning. Our moms mean so much.

If I could just write, "You are in my thoughts and prayers," and let Hallmark or American Greetings do the rest I would spend far less time sitting at my desk staring at a blank page. Because my *thoughts* on death are so complex, and my *prayers* are so skeptical. Seems *my* particular brand of thoughts and prayers may not be so helpful, and why am I bothering to send a card if not to be helpful—if not to be a comfort somehow?

I want to believe all the consoling slogans about death, the hopeful promises about life after. I *want* to believe in the

"New City" of the Bible—the jeweled walls, golden avenues, pearly gates—because I'm supposed to. But bling doesn't much appeal to me in *this* life. I can't imagine I'll love it in the next.

Jackson Browne writes of death, in "For A Dancer," as a song that he can't get out of his head, but is unable to sing. This resonates with me. Death is an earworm for me these days, but I cannot for the life of me sing the words back to you, or play the notes on my piano. I wish I could.

Hence, my stuttering on the page as I sit down to write these cards. Struggling to find the balance between saying too little— *You're in my thoughts and prayers*—to saying too much, and running the risk of saying precisely the *wrong thing*. I *can* empathize with my friends who are grieving the loss of their mothers; I just lost mine a few months ago. But to imply that I know exactly how they feel is reductive and presumptuous, and possibly not helpful at all. This is what we do though, in an attempt to empathize. We stake out some common ground and go from there.

Right before my mom died—or actually, as she was dying, I got a text from a friend in Georgia who had been going through her own struggles. Since my family and I were all gathered around my mom's bedside awaiting the awful inevitable, I wasn't able to return her text until the hospice nurse came in and gave us a break.

I went out in the hall and texted Tina back, letting her know what was going on, that Mom was very sick and probably down to her last few hours. She texted back that her mom was very sick, too. At that point, my siblings and I were called back to Mom's bedside, and I didn't get to respond to her sad news right away.

It was a very long night. Sometime around midnight, I did manage to text her back, asking how her mom was holding up.

Within minutes, I got the text, "She has diarrhea."

Hmmm. Seems "very sick" means different things to different people. It took all the restraint I could muster the following morning not to text, "So, how's your mom? Mine's dead."

Now, this little incident was more nuanced than I've described it. I suspect her texts, as many before, were the unfortunate result of tipsy texting. But my point is this: even when we're sure we know how someone feels, either because we've experienced or are currently experiencing something similar, we may be way off the mark. Diarrhea. Dying. They sound a little alike. And both do imply "sick." But, as you may have guessed, this brand of "empathy" was not particularly comforting to me. In fact, it would have infuriated me had it not been so darkly hilarious. Really, Tina, *really? Diarrhea?* (Put down the bottle, please.)

So, while drafting these notes to my friends who have recently lost perhaps the most important women in their lives, I'm careful not to even assume *that*. Maybe they couldn't stand her, or never really knew her. Or maybe she was their whole world right up until the end. Maybe she was so very sick, as mine was, that her death was something of a sad relief.

And those are the *easier* cards to write—the ones to mourners who have lost loved ones in the appropriate order. I struggled last month to write a note to a young friend of mine who had lost her little boy. Talk about the "vanity of words." Ah, the vanity of *everything*. I knew, beyond a shadow of a doubt, that there was not a single syllable I could scribble that would lighten her burden by even an ounce that day.

So why spend two and a half hours on a Sunday morning trying? Because I love her, and I must tell her that. In writing. Maybe she will revisit the stack of cards sent to her later, after the shock and horror have diminished a bit—as I have revisited the three stacks on *my* shelf—and know that she is cherished. And perhaps there will be a glimmer in her darkness, if only for that moment. Two and a half hours on a Sunday morning is worth it, just on the off chance. It's worth it to me.

But I must remind myself that even a quick stroll down the card aisle at Target and a few minutes at my desk with my "six-pack" are better than my characteristic, all-or-nothing approach to the difficult practice of expressing condolences. Even if I do default to the words pre-printed in the card and simply sign my name, it's better than nothing.

I remember sitting alone on my couch in late March, with a stack of ten or so cards in my lap after Mom died. I looked at the return addresses, and some were from friends across the country. Two were from friends I had not seen in years and years. I imagined these people, hearing of my loss, perhaps on Facebook, and making a mental note to send a card. Then, I could see them slowly perusing the card aisle at the grocery store or CVS, and they were thinking of *me*. That's all. They were thinking of me and wishing they could help me through my grief in some small way.

And they did. They do. It is always a good idea to connect. Even when you don't know what to say. And you probably won't. We usually can't know where our friends are in their grief. Platitudes and trumpet blasts of afterlife optimism may be premature. I love what Glennon Doyle Melton has to say about it: "The one closest to the departed has to be the first to step from despair to hope. Nobody else is allowed to jump ahead and shove open the door. That's the rule." (This in reference to her little boy and his dead fish, Jacob, but still.)

There is so much fear in the early stages of loss. What we have had—be it for decades or mere months—we no longer have. We don't know how to do without. I, for instance, had never known—not one minute of my 56 years—how to *not* have a mother on this earth with me. And though I had been independent for four decades, I still felt irrationally afraid after she died. How was I going to do this?

I like Deepak Chopra's advice on how to relate when someone else is in pain, "I won't be afraid of you, even though you may be afraid of your pain," and "You can have all the space you need, but I won't let you be alone."

So often we back away from those who are grieving. I once feigned a migraine (migraines are so easy to fake) to avoid going to the funeral of an aunt I loved. That was more than twenty years ago, and I still feel guilty about that. Maybe my six-pack is my penance. *I won't let you be alone.* You have this card. It may not be much, but it's something.

And something is better than nothing. And, yes, it *is* better late than never. And finally, (and this is for me) to quote Australian blogger Eva Young, *To think too long about doing a thing often becomes its undoing.* Nike had the best tagline of the 20th century: *Just do it.*

Do it. Imperfectly, awkwardly, "in bulk," if you need to. It doesn't have to be a card or a casserole or a bouquet of geraniums. But do something. Anything, if only to say, *I won't be afraid of you and your grief, and I will not let you be alone.*

I have three stacks of cards on my shelf in the office, and I know that I will need to make space for a fourth soon. Daddy is approaching his ninth decade on earth. His heart, we calculated, has beat more than three *billion* times. It is tired. *He* is tired.

Maybe I'll save one of my six-pack cards. Keep it for myself. *Wishing myself peace, healing, hope and everything my heart will need to get through this sad time.* It will need a lot. It has been cracked open and exposed to the elements a lot lately. It is weathered and weary. But that's the good thing about mourning, as Anne Lamott writes, "... grief ends up giving you the two best things: softness and illumination."

Maybe I will write in that card *today.* Tell myself that the new and excruciating grief I'm feeling will diminish with time and that my siblings and I will get through this. Together. And I will be able to pick up his stack, at some point in the future, and read calmly and with gratitude how much love is still available to me.

I will sign my card to me with love. I will address it to myself and place a stamp on the envelope, and on that day of grievous loss, when Daddy's soul departs his body, I will mail it to myself with my message.

Dear Sharla, you are not alone.

Sharla Dawn Gorder

~~Oh Most Holy Lamb of God on High~~
~~Our Father Who Art in Heaven~~
Hey God ...

I woke up the other morning with a prayer on my lips. Oh, yes, I did. That's just how holy I am.

Or not. Although my prayer did seem to lack the eloquence of, say Thomas Merton's *Contemplative Prayer*, or the vision of Sarah Young's *Jesus Calling*, it was from the heart, and in its way, quite comprehensive. It encompassed a lot.

I do admit, though, that it was also something of a lazy prayer, but you have to consider the source—the pray-*er*. That would be me, and I've been known to shirk a thing or two in my day.

Still it was a thorough prayer and sincere. I said:

Hey God,
Please take care of everything.
Let me know how I can help.

This prayer was not a joke. It was, in fact, a big improvement over previous prayers where I laid out all the details of my plan like an expense report to submit to God for approval and reimbursement. I don't think He likes that very much.

I'm not sure He likes this one any better, but I'm starting to believe that He isn't up there with a red pen grading my prayers anyway. (Heaven forbid I should offer up anything that merits less than a *B-*.) No, I'm thinking that all prayers are good prayers, as long as they are honest, as long as they are real. On both of those scales, this prayer would score an *A+*. Oh, wait, no one is grading.

I am not a succinct person—as anyone reading this book has already gleaned. If I can use sixteen really cool words to describe something that could be conveyed in six, I'll probably go for the most verbose option, because I just love the way words mess with each other in sentences. So for me to pare a prayer down to just 14 words is progress. (And the phrase "pare a prayer" is my point exactly. I love the alliteration, the rhyme—and I just used exactly 16 extra words to tell you that.)

Anyway, I had awakened feeling overwhelmed, as I sometimes do, and pathologically anxious, as I often do. I used to joke that it is as though a ragtag troop of gremlins set up camp every night at the foot of my bed. And at the moment they detect even a whisper of consciousness from me, they pounce. All 320 of them. Smelly, noisy, rude. Scrambling all over me like rats.

It's no wonder I woke up praying. And with so many varmints to contend with at once and on such short notice, there was just no time then to enumerate *all* of my woes. My short list was distressing enough: Mom was dying, my brother was very sick, the check-engine light on my car was on again, the rash on my elbow was back, my friend had insulted me, and I was constipated. There was more. But by the time I got to the gastrointestinal distress, I realized that He knew it all anyway, so why bother belaboring the obvious. And to God, it is *all* the obvious.

Hey God.

Please take care of everything.

Let me know how I can help.

One of my favorite writers, Anne Lamott, has pared it down even further. She professes to know little of God and prayer but has come to believe that our supplications are best kept simple:

Help. Thanks. Wow.

Ha! Three words. Never mind that she spent 102 pages elaborating. Her point is well taken and beautifully described. Humility, gratitude, and awe are all represented here in three little words. Again, very thorough. Very real. *A+.* (But who's grading?)

It has always puzzled me, though—that letter to the Thessalonians. The Apostle Paul urged us to *"pray without ceasing."* In order to do that, it would seem that I'd need a whole bunch of words. Not just 14. Certainly not just three. Even the Lord's Prayer (66 words) cannot be repeated *ceaselessly* without the words becoming rote and meaningless.

I don't understand prayer. But I find myself doing it anyway. I don't understand a lot of things, but I find myself flipping switches expecting the lights to come on, inhaling the air expecting my heart to keep beating, typing a clever message on my phone expecting my husband to read it and laugh. I pray, expecting to be heard.

And I'll be honest. I don't even always know *who* it is I think is listening. I know that is utter heresy; I'm sorry, Dad. But sometimes I just don't. I wish I did. *All the time.* I wish I had that kind of faith. But often, alas, *usually,* I don't. I pray anyway. Is that called faith or delusion? I don't know that, either.

During a particularly troubling phase in my life, I "prayed" aloud for an hour, out in the Gulf, alone on my paddleboard.

How holy, how sublime, you'd think. Only thing is, I had to pray as though I were *chatting*, and not with some supreme being on high. No, I spoke as though to my best friend, Vanessa, who had died suddenly a few months earlier.

I don't think God minded. Really, I don't. I just needed to take the intimidation out of my communication and add some comfortable familiarity; no one has *ever* felt intimidated or judged in a conversation with V. I told her everything I felt, just as though she were still with me, alive and joyous, gliding along next to me, celebrating the summer day. My soul needed to pray that way, I guess.

But there are also times when my soul cries out directly to that *Omnipotent Source of Power* that ostensibly runs the whole show. I have to confess that when I need a miracle, I can beseech with the best of 'em.

And I needed a miracle one terrifying night in April a couple of years ago. My prayer was: *DEARGOD DEARGOD DEARGOD DEARGOD PLEASE BRING THEM HOME ALIVE!!!*

They, on this particular night, had been reduced to two flickering points of light bobbing above the black Gulf of Mexico in an electrified midnight sky. The lightning storm came from out of nowhere, and it was among the worst in decades with a record-breaking 6,000 strikes in 15 minutes.

They, on this particular night, were my husband and three buddies, who had decided on the spur of the moment to take the kayaks out on what had first seemed to be a mild spring evening for a little moonlit red snapper fishing. At about 8:30 that night, the four of them set out on two tandem Hobie kayaks, equipped with pedals, outriggers, and even sails, destined to a favorite fishing spot some four miles out in the Gulf.

I had gone to a party a few houses down the beach, but by about 10:00, noticing the flashing skyline to the northeast, I started to get a little worried, and I headed back home. The call came a few minutes later as the storm pressed southward off the beach and into the Gulf.

It was not a drenching storm, nor a particularly windy one. But it was a savage storm and so potentially deadly that I could not venture even inches out onto my deck without fear of being instantly electrocuted. And my husband and friends were *out in the Gulf* in tiny yellow boats with tall masts—lightning rods really—pedaling for their lives.

Ted called—a miracle in itself that he was able to call me—and he spoke calmly, too calmly, and instructed me to get the powerful LED flashlight from the junk drawer, go to the top deck of the house and point it out to sea, to hold it there as a beacon, a lodestar for them to aim for as they pressed desperately toward shore. He told me that he loved me.

DEARGOD DEARGOD DEARGOD DEARGOD PLEASE BRING THEM HOME ALIVE!!!

Fifty-eight minutes of *DEARGOD DEARGOD DEARGOD DEARGOD PLEASE BRING THEM HOME ALIVE!!!* As I stood rigid, like a terrified Lady Liberty, torch held high, wrist pinned tightly between the door and the jamb, trying to shield all but my hand from the unrelenting lightning.

Between explosions, I could see two tiny lights bobbing helplessly above the sea maybe a mile out, and then the sky would fill with such blazing brilliance and noise that I'd be instantly blinded and deafened. The noise of this kind of thunder is no rolling rumble or bass-drum *boom*. No, it is a *CRACK* so loud and startling that I dropped my flashlight more than once and had to scramble a few feet onto the deck to retrieve it.

DEARGOD DEARGOD DEARGOD DEARGOD PLEASE BRING THEM HOME ALIVE!!! And keep me from frying, too, while you're at it.

And on this night, let me tell you, standing there alone in the doorway, I prayed as though I knew *exactly* who I was talking to: GOD. Capital "G". Sovereign One. Omnipotent One. I had no extra time to intellectualize, no extra emotion to dramatize, no extra words to trivialize. In order to remain standing there, I had to frankly *believe*—I can't even tell you now exactly *what* it was I believed in those frantic moments. It was all I could do just to pray. And to hold the torch.

Hey God.

Please take care of everything.

Let me know how I can help.

I guess that sometimes, maybe *usually*, I can believe that the first line of that prayer is a done deal. God, or Jesus, or Allah, or Spirit, or Universe or whatever handle I grasp, is going to *take care of everything*, one way or another. My challenge is always, has always been, in the *p.s.* of the prayer. *Let me know how I can help.*

Hold the torch, Sharla. Or lay with your Mom as she dies. Or tell him that he is right. Or get up and do the dishes. Or drive straight to her house without asking why. Or put down the bottle. Or put down the fork. Or pick up the phone and speak into it instead of text. Or quietly forgive. Or rescue the young dog. Or write the hard story. Or be very quiet when your ego is screaming. Or apologize, again. Or put your fingers on the keys of the piano, the strings of the guitar, the handle of the paintbrush. Walk. Run if you're able. Or be still. Very still, and *know* …

I believe there is a *knowing* that transcends words within me, within you. I can't tell you what it was I *knew* that night. But it was a part of me separate from my desperation, my intellect, even my imagination. Usually, I tend to be suspicious of the ineffable. I love to put things into words. But this, I cannot describe.

The storm worsened. I didn't think it was possible. I watched the two lights approach, so slowly, so *slowly* it seemed. But they were close now, maybe just a few hundred yards. And then the one on the right was gone. Suddenly extinguished in a piercing flash.

DEARGOD DEARGOD DEARGOD DEARGOD PLEASE BRING THEM HOME ALIVE!!! All of them, please.

I pointed the flashlight toward the remaining light and swept it to the right and left, frantic to find the other. I heard my teenage son and three friends come blustering into the house downstairs, having fled the storm themselves by car. I kept my vigil upstairs, desperate now to locate the other boat, but at this point the sky was so white with light—blinding, sizzling light—that it was all I could do to keep the one remaining mast beacon in sight between the paparazzi-ish assaults of glare.

The remaining boat was close now, close enough for me to make out the silhouette of mast—but I didn't know which boat I was guiding. The phone rang, and I dropped my flashlight again. Ted, breathless and desperate, said that he would need help bringing the boat in to shore. He and Brian had pedaled as hard as their legs would push against the storm for nearly two hours; they had no strength left to beach the boat. The boys would have to help.

Let me know how I can help.

Oh, but not this. Send my boy out there? (I seem to remember the story of another parent sending His son into a perilous situation—but I'm no *God*, thankyouverymuch. I believe we've already established that.)

Incredibly now, the storm was directly on top of the house. I thought I could smell burning quartz, as the sand on the beach was struck again and again. The teenagers, still jacked-up with adrenaline, were now faced with the prospect of running *into* an electrified minefield of a beach *toward* a 16-foot lightning rod attached to a boat floundering in the shore break.

Did they hesitate? Even when the lightning hit so close that it knocked Myles' buddy to his knees in the dune, they raced *away* from safety, toward the kayak. I held the torch for the other boat that I could no longer see and watched. It took all four boys to drag the two men ashore.

And then, suddenly, the other boat was visible—*from the opposite direction*. Impossible. The other mast light that I had watched earlier had been quite a distance to the *east* of Ted's boat. This one came from many hundreds of yards to the *west*, an impossibility considering the winds and tides. But there it was. And the boys, the two exhausted men, and now the dog, too, all scrambled back *into* the fray and over the dune, to haul in the second boat.

OH, THANKYOUGOD, THANKYOUGOD, THANKYOUGOD. Simultaneous with WOWWOWWOW, number three. Help—*check*. Thanks—*check*. Wow—*check*.

The men collapsed wild-eyed and spent, on the sofa on the covered porch. The silence for the first couple of minutes was eerie. The storm had abated, but the *Wow* remained. *What just happened? And how are we still alive?*

And where is that eastern boat? The one that escorted Ted's kayak to within sight, then disappeared. Wow.

Maybe it's the *Wow* that keeps me praying—that punctuating astonishment in the wake of a "miraculously" answered prayer, or simply in the softly exhaled wonder—*wow*—in the glow of another sublime sunrise. Or maybe it's just a good, wholesome habit, like making my bed; I was taught to do it when I was little, and I'm compelled to do it still, now that I'm big. I don't know.

Mark Nepo writes, "If you try to comprehend air before breathing, you will die." Prayer feels that way to me. Air is air, as prayer is prayer. Doesn't matter if it's a gale-force prayer—as in DEARGOD DEARGOD DEARGOD DEARGOD PLEASE BRING THEM HOME ALIVE!!!—or a barely perceptible breeze of a prayer—Dear God, please take care of everything. Let me know how I can help—it's all good. A+.

God is great. God is good. Wow.

Sharla Dawn Gorder

More

God is slippery. Or maybe it's just that my hands are always wet. But right when I think I've got a hold, a grip on some spiritual truth or revelation, it slips away, and I'm left staring at my empty hands, or pulling my pockets inside out looking for the popsicle I thought I'd save for later.

Still, I pray. Still, I seek. Still, I sense that there truly is a divine unifying force at work in the world, even when I cannot feel it at work in *me*. Mark Nepo writes: "Here, the exquisite risk becomes the courage of heart not to forget, not to believe that the extraordinary center of things has vanished because we have lost touch with it."

And I lose touch, more often than I like to admit. Blame my slippery hands. My sticky pockets. My humanness can be such an inconvenience. Still I pray. And of late, my prayer has been crystallized down to five words—*God, reveal yourself to me.*

I first made this request while sitting in the sand at dusk, the irony of the glorious sunset over the Gulf not lost on me. If, indeed, God is implicit in nature, then, of course, there He is, right in front of me, all around me, within me. All the time. Why ask for more?

Ah, but that is what I do. Ask for more. Hasn't that always been my mantra—*more, more, more?* One more compliment, one more cookie, one more gold star, one more dollar, one more drink. And then maybe one *more* after that.

So, dolphins playing beneath radiant heavens on a deserted beach notwithstanding, I asked for *more* in the way of celestial revelations. Go figure.

I am a seeker. I read. I study. I write. I discuss. I pray. I wonder. I observe. I meditate. I analyze. I explore. I question. I listen. I ponder. I think.

I think. And I think. And I think. And then, of course, like the scarecrow on the way to Oz, I think some *more*.

Very early one Monday morning a while back—we had just "sprung forward" into daylight savings time—I was crossing the hall to wake Taylor for school, when out of the corner of my eye, I glimpsed the most striking, distinct shadow of a cross on the wall ahead of me to the left. The rising sunshine was pouring through the window over the landing casting the radiant image before me. It was so vivid. So lovely.

I love symbols. I revel in images and symbols and signs. I am a seeker. I am drawn to parables and allegories and metaphors. And there is perhaps no more evocative symbol for me than the cross. Having been brought up in a Christian home and community, the cross, not surprisingly, represented spirituality to me as a child and teen and still endures as a sacred symbol for me.

So, as I crossed the hall to Taylor's room, while I couldn't see the *actual* pewter cross on the chest of drawers around the corner, I could see the very vivid shadow it cast, as though the image had been painted with a very sure hand, directly onto the wall.

Did I mention that I like *more*?

Well, of course, I wanted to see *more* of this loveliness. I took a small step back, then a couple of steps forward, and it was gone.

Totally obscured at this point by my head. Undaunted, however, I did the little dance again, and alas, still my big ole bedhead got in the way. A third time I tried to reposition myself for a better look, and a third time, yes, you guessed it, *my head got in the way.*

My head gets in the way.

Well, duh.

Now at this point I could wax philosophical or poetic. I could recycle an old sermon from my years as a teenage evangelist. I could get really sentimental or bore you with flowery interpretations of the whole ten-second experience.

Or I could just say three things:

- ONE: I wasn't necessarily looking for an epiphany when I happened upon it. I was just doing what I do at 7:30 in the morning. However, I *had* opened myself to the possibility of spontaneous holiness in my life, simply by asking, and praying to be aware. *Reveal yourself to me.*

- TWO: The gift was just that. A present. And not amenable to manipulation, duplication or preservation. It was in a *moment.* Again, the *present* one. The present tense. The one I'm endeavoring to live in, and incidentally, the easiest one to conjugate.

- THREE: My head can tend to get in the way. I can overthink a *sneeze*—and totally lose it. I can turn a tender and lovely blessing into a rhetorical treatise that no one, least of all myself, understands. (Which is why I limited myself to three points here, probably three too many.)

And lest you think these bullet points occurred to me spontaneously, and I was instantly enlightened, the tale continues.

Four days later, still wanting *more,* it occurred to me that, although I was sure to write about this, don't you know, a *picture* is worth a thousand words.

So, bright and early Friday morning, armed with my iPhone, I stealthily approached the shadow-stained wall, knowing that some type of contortion would be called for if I was going to get my noggin out of the way long enough to snap a picture. And still, it seemed, no matter where I stood, some part of me got in the way, obscuring or otherwise contaminating the shot. I turned my phone this way and that, arched my body in and out of the light, stood on my tiptoes, and then crouched down low.

Finally, I had it! Perfect. After snapping the photo, I paused for a second to admire again the clarity of the icon on my wall. And I realized, with a start, that I was on my knees.

Hmmm.

I think it was Einstein, of all people, who is reported to have said, "There are only two ways to live your life. One is as though nothing is a miracle; The other is as though everything is." I choose B.

I recently read in a beautiful book by Deepak Chopra, "… you have the right to appreciate the patterns of connection that you've made." He even acknowledges, "…it may feel peculiar to do this." Kind of like the kid in that movie *The Sixth Sense* confessing, "I see dead people," it's sometimes awkward to let on that not only do I talk to God, sometimes he talks back. Maybe not in a booming baritone and a burning bush; that would freak me out. He talks to me in ways that I can understand. *In intimate ways specific to me alone.*

God, that's beautiful. And with *that* I'm finally understanding what that clichéd "personal relationship" with Christ or God, or Allah, or Krishna, or Ganesha, or whatever appellation I designate, can really mean to *me*.

So, the guidance gleaned from that shadow on my wall—even beyond the obvious cautionary lesson not to overthink God, and the reminder to remain ever humble in my quest—beyond even those rich, life-altering insights, the most beautiful thought remains: I am cherished. I am *that* loved. That sunrise on that wall at that moment rose for *me*. I am never forgotten, never ignored, never left *alone* to figure it out. I am a part of it *all*, and all of it is part of me.

God, reveal yourself to me. I want more.

And for once in my life, my compulsive nature serves me well. Funny how that works—how the most devastating aspect of my personality can also be the most liberating.

Yes, I chose B.

Everything is a miracle.

Jesus Pancake

A man in Ohio found Jesus. In his pancake. Or more accurately, *on* his pancake.

Mike Thompson of Beachwood, Ohio was flipping flapjacks one Saturday when he noticed the Son of God in his griddle. Right there, plain as can be, on little Susie's pancake—the long-haired, sad-eyed, bearded image of the King of Kings Himself.

Reportedly, Thompson and his wife were awed and humbled by their breakfast, and subsequently put the thing up for sale on eBay—opening bid $500. All the major networks carried the story, and I got to see the flapjack for myself. There it was—etched in non-stick cooking spray—the likeness of a scraggly-headed man. Jewish or Gentile, it's hard to say.

In fact, call me a heretic, but I was hard-pressed to affiliate the pancake with any specific race or religion. Could have been Charles Manson, or Osama Bin Laden, or anybody from Lynyrd Skynyrd. In the end, the only name I could confidently link to the pancake was Aunt Jemima.

But believers believe. That's what they do. The Virgin Mary has appeared as a watermark on a Chicago overpass, a grease stain in a Mexico City subway, and most famously (and lucratively) on a grilled cheese sandwich on Diana Duyser's nightstand. That's where she kept the thing, partially eaten, in an acrylic box by her bed, until she reportedly sold it on eBay for $28,000. (Really?)

You can also find Mother Theresa's mug reverently displayed under glass at a Texas diner—on a sticky bun. And it seems that Jesus is just as comfortable in the bathroom as he is in the kitchen: A family in Splendora, Texas invited the devout to worship a mildew stain in his image in their john.

Go figure. People need to believe. In something. In *anything* it seems, be it motor oil smeared on the concrete or Michelangelo's Pietà. Since the beginning of time, people have craved the attention of the Divine. And people will find God where they will. Who am I to judge?

I see God, too. Every day. Mostly in the faces of my children. Despite my innate skepticism throughout the years, I could not *not* believe when Tay-tay murmured in his sleep, "I love you, Mommy." Or when Myles, as a big, boisterous teenager, snuggled in next to me on the couch. I am forever reduced— or exalted, who's to say?—to an irrational, fanatical, born-again believer. Perhaps I *need* to believe to feel safe. But believe I do. In my own clumsy, wavering way. And believe I will.

But leave my grilled cheese sandwiches out of it.

OMG

At 6:43 this morning, I raced down the walkover to the beach in the freezing dawn to greet the sunrise, with only seconds left to spare. And in the same moment my toes touched the sand, the sun touched the horizon, spilling pink and orange, and even lavender light into the Gulf and sky and me. I found myself saying out loud—oh my God! And of course, my technologically habituated brain couldn't help but abbreviate it. *OMG*, I repeated. And I decided that I love that expression, that *OMG*.

I know that it is offensive to many—flirting with taking God's name in vain, I suppose. But in the context of the glorious rising sun, I think I felt the requisite reverence for it to qualify as true praise. And the thing I *really* enjoyed about that little three-word exclamation went even beyond the awesome subject (God). I loved the *pronoun*, the "my" in the OMG. *My* God. He is my God. Of course, it's lovely that he is yours, too. But in that moment, what delight I felt in calling Him mine, all mine.

Back in middle school, during my stint as an ersatz evangelist—actually, I was a "Jesus Freak" (hey, there are worse things to get freaky over)—I devoutly proclaimed the message of "salvation" to anyone who would listen, and a whole lot of folks who wouldn't. I employed some well-rehearsed Christian buzzwords in my spiel: *Your salvation lies in a personal relationship with Christ.* Or a personal relationship with God. And let's not forget the Holy Ghost. Whichever way, it was a *personal* relationship I was touting.

Except, somehow I got the idea that your "personal" relationship had to look exactly like my "personal" relationship—*my* concept of God: *my* preferred doctrine, dogma, scripture, music, prayers, leisure activities, and lifestyle in general. Basically, unless your "personal" God wasn't just like my "personal" God, tough luck, sucker. We'll pray for you.

Oh, and we did. We prayed and prayed for your poor, wretched soul. We had prayer meetings, prayer chains, even prayer workshops. We sang our prayers, and wrote our prayers, and whispered them desperately when we'd see you at the Piggly Wiggly buying Boone's Farm. *Oh, Lord, please show Kevin the joy of a personal relationship with you.*

And we, or at least *I*, never stopped to think about what I was preaching, for at the time I eschewed all reference books except the Bible. If I had spent a few minutes with *Mr. Webster*, however, I might have noticed that the word "personal" pretty much implies something "done in person without the intervention of another."

But at twelve-and-a-half, I was all about the intervention. *Time is running out! Jesus is coming! Better be ready!* I didn't want you to be left behind. Oh, no I didn't. And I wasn't content to simply counsel you privately at your locker between classes. No, no, no. There wasn't enough time. I had to reach a wider audience.

Audience. So, I wrote a play. A four-act play called *The Rapture.* I also cast, produced and directed the show which—and I can hardly believe it was allowed—was performed during school

OMG

hours before the entire student body of Gulf Breeze Middle
School in the spring of 1971. This was during the height of the
Jesus Movement counterculture of the late '60s and early '70s,
and I was gonna leave my mark.

Oh Lord. Arthur Miller I am not. But with all the passion and
conviction and time on my hands of a preteen who has yet to
discover boys, I earnestly presented my masterpiece to my peers,
hoping to save a soul or two from the heinous tribulation to
come and the eternal damnation to follow. All that Bible reading
made me something of an expert—or so I thought. *Move over,
Jesus. Maybe I'm "the way, the truth, and the light."*

The message of my play was not subtle. Basically, if you
smoked cigarettes, drank alcohol, or "cussed," you were doomed.
If you toted a Bible, went to Jesus rallies, and could recite John
3:16 in your sleep, you'd be fine. Being able to speak in tongues
was also a nice touch.

Okay, so I was twelve. And very lucky that those "thugs" in my
school who French kissed each other and smoked Virginia Slims
behind the rec center, didn't form a lynch mob after the first act
and come kick my holy hiney. But I bet they wanted to.

It's just human nature. It's really offensive to be preached at.
Some people can tolerate, even enjoy, being preached *to*. But
there's a subtle difference there. It's one thing for your spouse to
throw a tire iron *to* you if you get a flat tire on a deserted road.
Quite another for him to throw one *at* you. Different intent.
Different result.

Emphasis on *intent*, here. As an adult, I tend to run like hell
from anyone hurling tire irons at my head, though I am generally
open to those who approach me in a spirit of mutual discovery
and cooperation—*Here, I'll help you change that tire.* I don't think

I'm unique in that preference. While many of us do reach the point during periods of great grief or challenge where we think we just want someone to tell us what to do, that resignation rarely lasts. The human spirit is too curious, too creative, too *big*, to be confined to the parameters of any dogma, credo, or four-act play written by a twelve-year -old.

There's a reason that text shorthand *OYG* will never catch on. I don't know *Your God*. Even if you zealously and earnestly try to introduce me to *YG* with or without a tire iron in hand, we may never become more than casual acquaintances without that pesky "personalness" thing coming into play. It's my job to discover *MG*. My job. Back to Webster's take on it. Personal: *done in person.*

In person. Not *out* person. With*in*. And I risk a cliché here—it is, and forevermore shall be an *inside* job. With outside influences, to be sure (cue magnificent sunrise), but God cannot be imposed upon, inflicted on, or otherwise foisted upon your kids, your friends, your spouse or your 7th grade classmates. I know. I tried. I wrote a frickin' play!

Oh, I can just feel those heresy hackles rising out there. People probably want to yell at me. And slug me with their tire iron. Am I really saying that we shouldn't "witness" for Christ? Well, maybe we shouldn't, at least not in the way *I* did back in the day.

Thursday nights, after Bible Study, we'd go downtown in packs and preach salvation to the poor lost souls on Palafox. I remember after one particularly vigorous campaign, my brother and his friends were heading home and were pleasantly surprised and heartened to see a trio of raggedy young men on the corner of Chase and Spring Streets, enthusiastically pointing skyward, in the "One way to Jesus" gesture we Christians used to express our solidarity with Christ and one another. I'm sure my bro felt a keen satisfaction as he approached those men. Only to be quickly replaced with panic, as he found himself glaring into the headlights of an oncoming van. Damn, I mean *darn*, those one-way streets!

Which brings me back to the question of options. Could it be true, as I was taught, that there *are* no other options, that there *is* only *one way*, to spiritual transcendence? As you probably have guessed by now, I no longer believe that. That said, I would never let my Dad read this paragraph. He would be very sad—and troubled. He would be earnestly worried about my soul and the safety of his baby girl during all those famines, wars, plagues, beheadings, and general unpleasantries of the Tribulation—which could start as soon as Tuesday.

I recently read, "The world doesn't want to be saved; it wants to be loved. That's how we save it." This comes much closer to my grown-up opinions on the nature of God, or Allah, or Spirit, or Higher Power, or Universe, or whatever label I choose to attach to my belief in a benevolent over-arching life force accessible and relevant to me *personally*.

Daddy, please don't worry. I know this sounds like blasphemy to you. I *believe*, Dad, I *do*. But like the father exclaims to Jesus in that Bible story in Mark—the father who wanted more than anything to see his little boy healed—"I believe. Help my unbelief." All in the same breath, he proclaimed *and* confessed. He told the truth, *his* truth. And his boy was cured.

That's the story of my life I suppose, certainly the story of this book, the story of my stories: proclaiming and confessing. *Proclaiming* that I believe that this life is worth living enthusiastically, with kindness, humor, and compassion, and that I am never alone. *Confessing* that often I lose my connection and forget how to dial back in. And then I *feel* alone. But I *know* I am not. A paradox, sure. And I don't understand it and can't explain it, but there is a *knowing* for me that is neither purely cognitive nor emotional that transcends what I can think or feel, and simply *is*.

Years ago, in a Women's Group workshop, we were called upon to describe the characteristics of the God of our understanding. I took this assignment very seriously. At least at first. For extra credit (I love extra credit), I was encouraged to write a letter from God to myself, ostensibly to personalize (there's that word again) all of those attributes and see them in ways that were relevant to me in real life.

I felt stumped. Who am I to speak for God, much less write for Him? He's the most accomplished writer I can think of, if book sales are any indication. But I wanted to do the assignment. A friend suggested that I try writing the letter from the perspective of my most treasured *mortal* relationships, my relationship with my boys. Now, that I could do.

Sure enough, all of those qualities I had assigned to the God of my understanding formed the basis of my love letters to Myles and Taylor. Back to kindness, compassion, tolerance, hopefulness, helpfulness, forgiveness, love. Still, I have to confess that the idea of deliberately cobbling together a God I could relate to seemed simultaneously a little simplistic and a lot presumptuous to me.

I found myself wandering the aisles of *Build-a-Bear Workshop* in my imagination, in search of the perfect little god-toy to assemble, take home, and snuggle. And the options were limitless.

Why, my build-a-bear god didn't even have to be a bear! He could be a monkey, a ninja turtle, even a mermaid! I got to choose whether I preferred a firm or squishy god (squishy), and he could smell like a cupcake or even cotton candy. I settled on mint chocolate chip.

Choosing the voice of my god was a little more complicated. On the one hand, I wanted to feel safe and protected, so something James Earl Jonesy would have been nice. But I also might enjoy the friendly enthusiasm of a Casey Kasem voice or the soothing timbre of a Michael Bublé croon. Sadly, none of those was available.

So much to consider. And I didn't even have the chance to dress and accessorize the god of my creation before I lost interest in my Build a Bear metaphor. But let me just say—tidy whities or boxers? I would have had to choose.

And I wondered as I wonder now, do we *really* get to decide who God is? Probably not. But we do get to decide how we will respond to the spiritual stirrings of our souls. Absolutely. And not surprisingly, it turns out that I'd like to respond with all those characteristics I assigned to my God in the first place. Not the squishy, smooth talking, mint chocolate chip attributes. The other ones. The ones I love my children with.

The Dalai Lama said, "My religion is kindness." I'll drink *that* Kool Aid. Because with that simple doctrine comes kindness, compassion, tolerance, hopefulness, helpfulness, forgiveness, love—all of the things that move my spirit and make me want to be a better person.

And when I pray, I do address that spiritual presence as "God." Not because I've got God pegged. I don't. But simply because that's the way I learned to address Him. But (sorry Dad) I don't mind if you use another name, or even if you have no name at all. Some things are truly ineffable. *YG* may be one of them.

The sunrise this morning made me gasp, literally taking my breath away. I wish you could have seen it. Maybe you did. It rose the same for all of us. And I don't know about you, but I took it *personally*, as I often do, and whispered, "Oh my God."

OMG, TY.

Bye Now

Ba Dum Tshh!

Mother's Day, motherless—for the first time ever. In all of my 56 years, I've always had a flesh-and-blood mother to celebrate. Now, there are only ashes—"remains" they called them when I picked them up from the funeral home. But to me they just looked like ashes, nothing more and nothing less. What *remains*, Mom's *remains*, as it were, are not in a plastic box, but in me.

As maudlin as that might seem, and as difficult as it was to write that sentimental sentence, the idea is not trite. It is the only thing that makes sense to me. Whatever *remains* of Mom must be carried on by me and my siblings. And I want to carry on the best of her and forgive the rest, so that my boys will have something good of me on *their* first Motherless Day.

These are Mom's true remains:

- Kindness: I will be good to people. I will listen patiently with calm attention. I will hold a place for them.
- Humility: I will stand gratefully beside—never above—my friends and family, and I will drop to my knees before them whenever necessary.
- Generosity: I will give graciously of my time, my attention, my money, my love. I will share the best of all I have. Every day I will give something away.

- Loyalty: I will be steadfast. Devoted. Never demeaning. I will cooperate instead of compete. I will be counted on.
- Gentleness: I will not be harsh or rough with anyone. I will treat all respectfully, tenderly—like a newborn kitten maybe, or a perfect sand dollar.
- Humor: I will see the irony in things. I will appreciate laughter—even when on this, my first Mother's day without Mom, it would seem that tears are more in order.

About a year before Mom died—but many years into the dark dementia that eventually took her life—we were sitting together on a shady bench in the courtyard of her assisted living facility. By this point in her decline, Mom wasn't talking much. Language was hard for her. But on this mild, spring day, she was *inspired*, or so it seemed. (Inspired by the love of her life—my Dad. For 70 years he had been her accomplice, and a few months later, at the very end, even when she no longer remembered how to sit up in her bed or swallow her food, she remembered how to tilt her chin up when he approached to receive his kiss.)

On this warm, sweet afternoon there on that bench under the magnolia tree, Mom had a twinkle in her eye. She spied Daddy shuffling up the sidewalk toward us with the mail.

She blurted out, "Sharshee, I wouldn't trade that man for Rock Hudson."

I laughed and said, "Well, that's a good thing, Mom, because, he's gay."

Without hesitation Mom said, "Yeah, and dead."

Ba dum tshh! Cue rimshot!

She never lost her sense of humor. Even months later, as she lay on death's door after we brought her back from the hospital on hospice care to die at home.

In one rare moment of consciousness that first week, my brother—my dear, gentle brother—brushed the hair back from Mom's tiny face and told her how happy he was to see her.

"We almost lost you, Mom," he said. "You were very sick."

She had been mostly comatose for weeks now, but without hesitation, she looked at him, deadpan and said, "Ah, sorry to have missed that."

Ba dum tshh!

Ba dum tshh! Mom. I love you.

Sharla Dawn Gorder

I am Sand

Early November, I walked the shore at dawn with Shuba. The seashells on the beach were so broken up—crushed actually—by the recent storms, that they kind of felt good under my feet. Almost like scratching an itch I didn't know I had. I still like the broken ones.

I walked east in the crunchy sand toward my daily rendezvous with the sunrise. A robe of gray flannel clouds cloaked the horizon. I suspected He would be late. We were scheduled to meet at 6:05 a.m. sharp. Sometimes He is late. He can get away with it. He is God. He gets away with lots of stuff.

I turned back toward the house enjoying the feeling of the shells between my toes, the sight of Shuba jamming her snout into crab holes, the murmur of the Gulf, now finally relaxing after too many storms. And then, I felt some pink in the air (Yes, you can feel the color of a sunrise even before you see it), and I looked back.

6:05 a.m. Magenta rising. My favorite. In the big box, the Crayola 64, magenta was always my favorite color. Light broke the dark horizon line in a glowing pink arc. And then it was gone, shrouded behind the heavy drape of clouds.

But it rose for *me*, and showed itself for a moment to *me*—this broken girl at dawn on the shore.

Daddy died on a Friday. We weren't expecting it; we *were* expecting it. We weren't ready; we were ready. We were distraught; we were relieved. For 17 days we stood vigil at the hospital, my sister and brother and me, silently begging him to live even as we fumbled to find a pen so we could sign the permission slip that would excuse him from this life. His last days in that mechanical bed were truly awful. Even at 88, he did not give up without a fight. When he died, Jem stood in the middle of the room like a bewildered orphan and said, "The roof is gone." Mom and Dad were *both* gone now, one right after the other it seemed.

Daddy's memorial was held in his assisted living facility, and we sang that old Peaches and Herb song—*Reunited*. In 70 years, Mom and Dad had never been apart for more than a few days when Daddy had to travel for business. I guess Daddy decided that eight months was just too long. He had to go.

We had a second memorial for Daddy in a little clearing on a piece of farmland in his hometown. We planted a fig tree. Old friends and relatives gathered around and told stories. My cousin, Todd, read a poem. As soon as he read the title, *To be of Use*, my heart nearly burst with kinship and love. How did he know? He had only seen my Daddy a couple of times in the last couple of decades. How did he understand Daddy's ultimate passion, his *raison d'être?*

This is truly all my Daddy wanted—*To Be of Use*. The poem is by Marge Piercy, and though she didn't know it, she wrote it about James M. Sullivan Sr. She wrote it about my Dad.

Todd stood by the little sapling and in a quavering voice began to read about my Daddy who loved the land and the work of the land that is "common as mud," who strained in that mud "and the muck to move things forward … to do what has to be done again and again."

That was Daddy. In work, he was a farmer, planting forests of trees he knew he would never see grow tall. In love, he was my mother's caregiver till the very end of her dementia and her life. In spirit, he loved and served the God of his understanding with unflagging devotion and child-like enthusiasm even till the awful end, when *I, myself*, was furious with God for allowing this devoted disciple to suffer so. (I'm still a little ticked.)

Percy's poem ended with the words: "The pitcher cries for water to carry/and a person for work that is real." And when Daddy's real work on Earth was done—his farmlands tended by his boy, his bride in the arms of Jesus Himself, and God's message of redemption offered to every soul he encountered—his body died, a vessel emptied out and used up, to a good and holy purpose. And his spirit moved on.

I miss his big farmer's hands. I regret the times when I would visit and pull my hands away from his before he was ready. He'd playfully clasp tighter as I began my goodbyes after lunch. Usually, I would stay another moment or two, then unlace our intertwined fingers, kiss him on the top of the head, and leave. The last time I held his hands, the hour of his death, he gripped my right hand so tightly that I couldn't pull away. He clutched my sister's hand in his left. And then—how did it happen like that?—he let go. His grip slackened. I remember *that* more than the absence of breath or of heartbeat, though my head was on his chest, ear pressed to his heart. He let go of my hand before I let go of his. He had to, I suppose. It was the first time. It was the last time. I'm trying not to blame him for that.

I can be a little whiney about things like that. Daddy loved to tell the story of the time (I must have been about four) when I climbed to the top of the swing set at the little park by our house. I'm not sure how I got up there all by myself, but Daddy was only a few yards away when he heard me hollering, and looked up to see me dangling from the crossbar. He ran to rescue me but, alas, I couldn't hold on. In the car on the way to the hospital for stitches, I wailed, "Daddy, why didn't you catch me? You should've run faster!"

And I still want him to be there for me. I've never known it any other way. But I'm a big girl now, and I know that it's my turn *to be of use* and to do *what has to be done again and again*, and to try to catch people when they're falling, and to hold their hands, and to tell them happy news about God, and to love them through their very best and their very worst.

It seems like a lot. But Daddy never complained, and neither will I.

The sun rose this morning for Shuba and me, though it seemed more reluctant than usual. That mattress of clouds at the horizon complicated things. Sometimes things are complicated. But still the sun rises. Life goes on.

Grief is complicated. I would think it would be familiar by now, and thereby easier for me. I've done this sad dance over and over the last couple of years. Jenna, Vanessa, Mom and Dad. Aren't you supposed to get good at things with practice? Ah, maybe I am. I *will* say that I am less afraid, less cynical, less resistant. I've read that grief is the price we pay for love. I love deeply. I grieve deeply.

And I am broken this morning—crushed, like those shells in the pink dawn light. I miss my father. I miss my mother. I fear I will be sand soon. But that's okay. Maybe I will become the gorgeous white quartz sand that this island is famous for.

Bring a pail and a little shovel. You can build a castle out of me on the beach. I don't mind. In fact, I think I'd like that. Let me *be of use* in some small way.

And the beat goes on. Thanks, Daddy.

Sharla Dawn Gorder

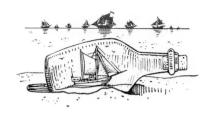

Every Ship that Sails

No sand castles today. Crazy storms all week brought the water right up to the walkover, and the beach is flat and unyielding. Shuba and I headed out just before sunrise and stopped at the edge of the wooden path that overlooks the shore.

The beach was a vast, white, featureless plateau, unmarred by a single footprint or track. The angry storm surge yesterday ironed out every divot, every dent. It was beautiful in a way, but kind of eerie. We stepped into the sand, and it was as hard as concrete. It surprised Shuba and she looked up at me in that quizzical, head-cocked way that dogs do, then bounded off down toward the water in search of ghost crabs to torment.

I took it all in. There was a time when a beach scene as desolate as this one seemed romantic to me. I was a moony-eyed teenager then. I didn't value footprints. I scoffed at the tourists who made them. I wanted the beach all to myself. To brood. Ha! That was back when I had nothing real to brood about.

Now that I do, I want those footprints back. I need evidence of life, of love, of people. And while I perhaps enjoy solitude more than most, I know that I *need* fellowship, friendship, kinship— every ship that sails. I need you all.

When I wrote in my journal all those years ago that "disconnection is fatal," I was terrified by my own realization.

Isolation has always been my default mode, especially when distressed. Believe it or not, I'm something of an introvert by nature. Hard times leave me longing for the underside of my bed. It's cool there. And dark. And no one can find me.

The times I don't *want* to be found are the times I am in most need of a caring search party. I have lain there motionless under that bed with my secrets, holding my breath, watching the shoes of concerned family and friends come so close to my hiding place, then amble away. A single audible exhale could have saved me. But I was stubborn in my shame.

I have often pondered the saying, "You are only as sick as your secrets." That's a powerful message, but for me, it doesn't go far enough. I have been even *sicker* than my secrets. That's what shame will do to you. It's the hard crust that seals in the festering mess, allowing a common illness, like a sore throat, to have carte blanche to rage and rage inside the damp darkness and to develop into a double bacterial pneumonia kind of sickness that kills you if left untreated.

Telling these stories is my treatment, maybe even my redemption. It connects me with you.

So, now you know. I am glad that you know, even if you admire me less for my weaknesses. That's okay. I just couldn't hold my breath any longer. I finally exhaled. Just one person heard at first. Ted lovingly pulled me from underneath my bed, from underneath my shame. He helped me up off the floor and we walked out of that sick room together and rejoined the world, which, to my surprise, was still in progress.

Rumi says, "There are a thousand ways to kneel and kiss the ground, there are a thousand ways to go home again." There are a thousand ways to tell your story, to get yourself back to a beach with footprints, and it can start with something as simple as a sigh, an exhalation that at least one other soul can hear.

Or, you can scream and flail and make a scene. That works, too. I remember being lost and alone on my paddleboard in a coastal marsh on the East Bay a couple of years ago. It was getting dark, and I was getting panicked. Ted and I were out camping with a group of friends from his kayak club at a beautiful site near the mouth of the Yellow River. I had taken the board out for a little meditative paddle before supper.

It was a warmish spring evening, and the water was calm. I paddled upstream just a few hundred yards and turned left into a narrow little inlet—no more than six feet across—bordered by sawgrass. I rowed slowly down the slender path and glided into the marsh. The view was stunning. The pond was so still and reflective that the mossy oaks on the shore seemed to be on the water with me. The light was low and pinkish-orange. I could smell salt, and rot and a comforting waft of campfire smoke. I wasn't far from "home."

I sat down cross-legged on my board in the middle of the marsh and took it all in. Emerson said, "Nature always wears the colors of the spirit." Ah, well she was dressed to impress that evening. I was mesmerized. I closed my eyes and drifted.

I don't know how long I floated there enraptured, but something jolted me from my reverie—a small splash maybe, or a distant heron call—and I saw that the coral light had grayed, and the shadows had lengthened. The smell of campfire had gotten stronger.

I stood up with my paddle and began to stroke toward the nearest little channel leading back toward the bay. I didn't remember it being this narrow—barely wider than my board in places. Tall cordgrass crowded and defined both sides of the path. No, this couldn't be right. I paddled backwards until I was back in the marsh. I looked around for another outlet in the fading light and hurried over to it. This one was a little broader at the start but quickly tapered down to nothing. The third outlet I tried ended so abruptly that my board got jammed in the muck and the grass, and I had to get off of my board and into the sludge in order to pull it back into narrow canal.

Everything was now slate colored. Pretty light all gone. Back in the middle of the marsh, I looked toward land and considered abandoning my board if I could see a way to wade to shore through the shallow swampland. But between the open pond and wooded shore, the teeming tract of thick and tangled vegetation was too dense to navigate on board or on foot. (And maybe I just heard a gator bellow. Maybe one I had awakened when I got off my board in his lair a few minutes earlier.)

Now, I could not only *smell* the blazing campfire, but I could also *see* it in the dying light. I was that close. The little campsite was just there, a few hundred yards back. They were roasting a pig. I could see the fire.

I, however, had no fire; my fellow campers could not see *me*. All I had was a board and a paddle. And a voice.

I used all three. After a brief temper tantrum (you ever seen anyone wail and stomp their feet on a paddle board?) I swallowed my pride and started screaming and waving my paddle in the air, as high as I could reach. The response was almost immediate. Dim figures in the distance began scrambling on the shore, launching kayaks, hurrying my way.

By the time Jay and Matt—two of my fellow campers—got to me, I was sitting cross-legged on my board again, relieved and embarrassed. And safe.

Safe. I was safe. Never mind that I got a little ribbing when we got back to camp. Never mind that I was offered an escort every time I ventured more than ten yards from my tent. I was safe. I had a voice. I hollered for help. Help came. I survived.

And that's not the only moral of this story. Another one came retrospectively. Later, after supper, side by side in our sleeping bags, Ted and I talked. I told him how scared and confused I had been, how frustrated I had felt when I couldn't find a way out. How I had paddled frantically from one canal to another, only to dead-end with the gators and snakes.

Ted was quiet for just a second, then he said, "You know, Sharla, you might have tried being still for a minute, just laying down on your board. The current—though you couldn't see it or feel it—was still flowing beneath the surface, and it was flowing toward open water. And that's where you wanted to go."

Well, duh. "Be still, and know ..." Stillness would have delivered me to the mouth of the right outlet, and I could have paddled home. And again, as in many ah-ha moments in my life, a James Taylor song serenaded me from the inside of my head. "*Look up from your life,*" he crooned. Yes, *there's always a river running under my feet*—or my board—even when I can't feel it, see it, or even imagine it. It is there, *ancient and sweet*, and it's *on its way back home*. I can always hitch a ride. Back home.

Home is where the footprints are.

I need footprints. I looked out over the beach behind the house this morning. It looked so desolate in the aftermath of all those storms. And at first glance, it *did* seem restful and sublime. But it was hard beneath my feet and barren. Even the crab holes were gone, and Shuba was devastated. Still, we put our paws in the sand and started walking toward the sunrise. And that's just what I have to do, put one paw in front of the other and move toward something lovely. There is always something lovely.

You are something lovely. You soften the sand beneath my feet, and let me know that we are all on this beach together, strolling toward another sunrise. I know we are. I can see your footprints even when I can't see *you*.

Aw—Don't be sad that it's over.
We can still be friends!

Visit me at Sharladawn.com
and get a brand new story, for free, every week!